Celtic Symbolism

The Ultimate Guide to the Spiritual Meaning of Symbols of the Celts and Their Use in Paganism

© Copyright 2024 - All rights reserved.

The content contained within this book may not be reproduced, duplicated, or transmitted without direct written permission from the author or the publisher.

Under no circumstances will any blame or legal responsibility be held against the publisher, or author, for any damages, reparation, or monetary loss due to the information contained within this book, either directly or indirectly.

Legal Notice:

This book is copyright protected. It is only for personal use. You cannot amend, distribute, sell, use, quote or paraphrase any part, or the content within this book, without the consent of the author or publisher.

Disclaimer Notice:

Please note the information contained within this document is for educational and entertainment purposes only. All effort has been executed to present accurate, up-to-date, reliable, and complete information. No warranties of any kind are declared or implied. Readers acknowledge that the author is not engaging in the rendering of legal, financial, medical, or professional advice. The content within this book has been derived from various sources. Please consult a licensed professional before attempting any techniques outlined in this book.

By reading this document, the reader agrees that under no circumstances is the author responsible for any losses, direct or indirect, that are incurred as a result of the use of the information contained within this document, including, but not limited to, errors, omissions, or inaccuracies.

Your Free Gift
(only available for a limited time)

Thanks for getting this book! If you want to learn more about various spirituality topics, then join Mari Silva's community and get a free guided meditation MP3 for awakening your third eye. This guided meditation mp3 is designed to open and strengthen ones third eye so you can experience a higher state of consciousness. Simply visit the link below the image to get started.

https://spiritualityspot.com/meditation

Or, Scan the QR code!

Table of Contents

INTRODUCTION 1
CHAPTER 1: THE ANCIENT CELTS 3
CHAPTER 2: CELTIC BELIEFS AND SYMBOLISM 13
CHAPTER 3: A-Z OF CELTIC SYMBOLS 22
CHAPTER 4: THE CELTIC TREE CALENDAR 43
CHAPTER 5: THE OGHAM ALPHABET 60
CHAPTER 6: THE WHEEL OF THE YEAR 80
CHAPTER 7: THE TREE OF LIFE 93
CHAPTER 8: ANIMALS AS CELTIC SYMBOLS 102
CHAPTER 9: CELTIC DIVINATION 111
BONUS: TREE MEDITATIONS 121
CONCLUSION 130
HERE'S ANOTHER BOOK BY MARI SILVA THAT YOU MIGHT LIKE.... 132
YOUR FREE GIFT (ONLY AVAILABLE FOR A LIMITED TIME) 133
REFERENCES 134

Introduction

The ancient Celtic culture has been attracting the attention and curiosity of people for centuries due to its rich traditions, fascinating mythology, and deep connection to nature. The Celts were a diverse group of people inhabiting various parts of Europe, and they left behind a rich legacy of symbolism that holds profound meaning to this day. This book explores the deep and captivating realm of Celtic spirituality and symbolism and teaches a few things about the Celtic heritage and its significance. Apart from spirituality, the Celtic culture is a complicated tapestry woven with intricate threads of music, art, folklore, and mysticism.

Although the Celts are mainly considered Irish people, they were also inhabitants of Scotland and Wales. They are most well-known for their deep affinity for the natural world, their sacred reverence for the cycles of nature, and the spirits that reside within this world. The vibrant festivals and celebrations held by the Celtic people attract the most attention from outsiders, but the mysterious symbolism makes this culture great. Symbols have played a central role in Celtic spirituality and served as the primary way the Celts communicated with the divine. Each symbol has a spiritual significance and a deeper meaning behind it.

To understand and unravel the mysterious world of Celtic symbolism, one must first acknowledge the significance of the natural world in Celtic spirituality. Paganism and its ties to nature, the earth, the natural elements, and spirits form the cornerstone of Celtic spirituality. For instance, with its strength and long life, the mighty oak tree represents wisdom and endurance, while the flowing rivers and sacred springs symbolize life's natural cycles. The Celts believe that the beautiful interplay of these elements is essential to uncovering the deeper mysteries of this world.

The intricate knots and spirals in Celtic symbols, also known as Celtic knots, hold special meaning in terms of spirituality. The interwoven lines and circles are representative of the interconnectedness of all things and the eternal nature of life. Although aesthetically interesting, Celtic symbols are not simply decorative motifs but representative of deeper spiritual meanings with themes of unity, eternity, and divine mysteries. The Celts truly believed that studying these intricate patterns would help them unlock the deeper layers of this world.

Studying Celtic symbolism won't just give you a glimpse into the worldview of the ancient Celts and their rich cultural heritage, but it will also help you connect with their spiritual practices. However, as you approach this exploration, it's essential to be sensitive and have an open mind to the various beliefs discussed in this book. Whether you go through Celtic mythology or the meanings behind Celtic symbolism, you should approach the subject with a sense of curiosity instead of being judgmental or skeptical. While it's okay to be skeptical, it's unacceptable to mock a culture, religion, or its beliefs. So, open your mind and heart to the mysteries that lie ahead, and let the world of Celtic spirituality captivate you.

Chapter 1: The Ancient Celts

It is believed the ancient Celtic culture originates from different tribes who once inhabited the territories of Western and Central Europe from 700 B.C.E. to 400 C.E. Initially. These tribes shared a common language, culture, and religion. However, after migrating to various parts of the world and bringing along their rich heritage and culture, they began to create greater diversity among the Celts. The rise of the Roman Empire suppressed most of the Celtic culture from several territories. However, it still survived in remote parts of Europe, including Ireland and England, where it is still practiced. This chapter explores the culture, society, art, religion, warfare customs, burial practices, and other aspects of the lives of the ancient Celts.

People often relate the Celts to the United Kingdom (mostly Ireland and Scotland).
OxYm3rioN, CC BY-SA 4.0 <https://creativecommons.org/licenses/by-sa/4.0>, *via Wikimedia Commons:* https://commons.wikimedia.org/wiki/File:Celts_in_Europe-fr.png

Who Were the Ancient Celts?

Due to a lack of historical records, the exact origin of the Celts is still debated among historians. Over the centuries, much of the ancient Celtic history was lost – and what is known of their culture has been pieced together from oral traditions passed down through generations and surviving examples of their intricate art.

The ancient Celts were a cluster of tribes who spoke the Celtic languages and lived during the Iron Age. Historians believe the Celts originated from the Hallstatt culture, which can be traced through records and findings from the Bronze and early Iron Ages artifacts. Over time and due to different circumstances, the Celts populated multiple European territories, including modern-day France, Italy, Germany, Poland, Spain, and Britain. After their dissemination, the Celtic tribes were divided into groups such as the Gauls, the Britons, the Gaels, the Celtiberians, the Galatians, and others – creating a great diversity amongst the tribes and making it harder to define their cultural structure. Moreover, the tribes often engaged in warfare with the Romans, who held much of the recorded history of the Celts – but it was colored with biased misunderstanding due to the conflict at the time.

By 300 B.C.E., the Celtic tribes inhabited most of Europe. After the Romans began a campaign against the Celts, and slowly started to destroy many of their civilizations on the mainland of Europe. Initially, the Romans attempted to invade Celtic Britain. However, they could not conquer many of the islands, or the far northern regions, where the Celts had managed to establish their new home. To this day, cultural traditions in Ireland, Scotland, and Wales can be traced back to the ancient Celts.

Celtic traditions still exist in other parts of Europe, including the Asturias region of Northern Spain. The Celts who lived there became the Galatians, and the survival of their traditions in Asturias means that today, they share many cultural commonalities and cultural heritage common with Celtic regions like Ireland and Scotland.

Celtic Societies

In the absence of first-handwritten records, it's almost impossible to discern the exact structure of the ancient Celtic society. That said, from the writing of diligent Roman authors, it can be concluded that Celtic tribes followed a hierarchical system that allowed them to maintain

stability in their communities. This hierarchical system likely had the following classes:
1. **The rulers and elite warriors** – A limited layer of society with many privileges and duties.
2. **Religious leaders and the Druids** – The living repositories of the Celtic community's collective knowledge. They were also exempt from paying taxes or partaking in military service.
3. **The specialized workforce of society.** These included craft workers, farmers, traders, and slaves. This was the largest group comprising less educated individuals.

Another fascinating fact about the Celtic society was how they treated women. Historical evidence suggests that there were several female chiefs in Celtic Britain and many monarchs, as well. These powerful women were responsible for ruling tribes and leading them into battle. In Celtic societies, men and women received equal treatment for elaborate burial rites and offerings. Archeological findings prove that the same amount of possessions depicting high status was buried with male and female leaders of many Celtic tribes.

Iron Age Celtic society was structured around the monarchy. After the society was split into different tribes, each was led by its own king. However, they were also high and low kings – both of which were elected under a tanistry system. The tanistry system was a long-standing custom amongst Celtic tribes, particularly in Ireland and Scotland, but it evolved and eventually changed into the feudal system, which determined the firstborn son as the family successor.

Over time, the ruling system changed to include elected chiefs and officials. Some tribes also had a small council of elders responsible for making the ruling decisions in their community. Often, two or more separate Celtic tribes would merge for mutual assistance and benefit. As a result, one or both of the tribes depended on each other for resources and ruling systems. However, the merger was often necessary due to the impending advancement of the Romans and the threat they posed to the Celts.

Celtic aristocrats used the patronage system they established with their followers to uphold their distinguished and often highly coveted status. They would offer their supporters hospitality, monetary support, different rewards, and legal protection in exchange for labor and the product of this. They were also expected to follow the aristocrats into battle and protect them when necessary. Celts of the highest status had clients from different classes. Sometimes chiefs and kings of lower rank would work with aristocrats with a higher social status and power.

The Celtic monetary system was mostly based on a simple bartering system. This involved exchanging items and services between two or more people without money. While this was a huge part of Celtic society, it also believed that the Celts used some form of proto-money. The Celtic ring money is the most commonly referenced currency among the Iron Age Celts. Gold and copper rings were the common currency in the system using ring money. These rings were often worn on clothing or tied together using ropes to facilitate their exchange of goods and services. Besides the ring money, bronze bells and axe heads also served the purpose of an early currency.

Culture and Religion

Celtic cultural markers varied significantly across the different tribes. All of these tribes were collectively labeled as "Celts," which some modern historians consider problematic because the tribes in the different parts of the world didn't follow a unified tradition. They existed separately in scattered territories, and the Celtic culture spread and evolved with time. It changed most dramatically during the European Iron Age due to their interactions with other cultures and belief systems and continued migrations. Initially, they probably had the same cultural background, beliefs, and customs. However, once they became scattered so widely that the tribes weren't even in direct contact with one another, they had fewer and fewer cultural elements in common.

Historians advise that the Celtic culture originated from three main cultural groups closely related to one another. These groups had the prominent Indo-European facets the Celtic culture (and several other European Pagan cultures) is based on. The first group, the Urnfield culture, can be traced back to the late Bronze Age. They are named after their widespread practice of storing the cremated remains of their dead in urns or burying the urns with the remains. Although there's a lack of archeological evidence proving the existence of this group, this tradition was later widely adopted by Celtic tribes. Ironwork became more prominent after transitioning from the Bronze Age to the Iron Age. This was evidenced in the changes in Celtic culture as well.

Named after the birth site of their original tribe in Upper Austria, the Hallstatt culture quickly scattered through Europe, conquering territories like Switzerland, Austria, Germany, France, and Bohemia. The quick dispersion of this culture across Europe is attributed to factors like trade, marriages, tribal alliances, and migration. It's also known that these tribes had an abundance of salt, iron, and copper deposits – and mastered how to trade these through the waterways. For example, they brought their goods to the Mediterranean and exchanged them for gold and amber jewelry. This is underlined by the amount of these foreign items found in the Hallstatt burial mounds. Unfortunately, due spread of other cultures and tribes and competition, the pool of resources was ultimately depleted, leading to the demise of the Hallstatt culture, which died out at the beginning of the 5th century B.C.E.

The third cultural group linked to the roots of the ancient Celtic culture is the La Tene culture, named after their presumed area of origin in Switzerland. This group of tribes was probably the most diversified of all three cultures. There were, however, some similarities to the other two cultures in art, religion, and language. The influence of the La Tene culture spanned Western and Central Europe, from Ireland to Romania. Several aspects of the everyday life of these groups made their way into the lives of future Celtic tribes, including ironworking, swirling-styled art, offerings made in water, and weapon deposition in tombs.

Among all the later Celtic tribes, the Galatians and the Britons were the two most prominent in establishing the basis of the Celtic culture. The Galatians lived in the Asturias region (northern Spain in modern times). This tribe had successfully fought off invasion attempts from both the Romans and the Moors. The Moors were spreading to the nearby regions at the time and already ruled much of current-day southern Spain. Celtic Galatian traditions have a huge part in Celtic celebrations and rituals. Cultural features of the Galatian tribes resembled earlier Celtic culture a great deal, with many similarities in art and symbolism. For example, the Galatian tribes often partook in traditions involving musical instruments similar to the ones used by Celtic tribes in other parts of Europe, particularly in Ireland and Scotland.

Britons and Gauls, the other two later Celtic tribes, initially settled in Northwestern France (modern-day Brittany). Since they were more isolated than Celts in other parts of Europe, other cultures didn't threaten these tribes, and they managed to retain most of the culture of their ancestors. Many festivals celebrated can be traced back to ancient

Celtic customs of honoring nature and deities. While the Romans did not initially manage to invade the Britons, they later succeeded in their attempts, pushing the Britons to the islands near Wales and Cornwall and north to Scotland.

The languages of the ancient Celts stemmed from the Celtic culture. Some of these languages are still in use today, like Welsh. Approximately a million people worldwide speak Welsh, while other languages, like Cornish, have fewer speakers.

Warfare and Craftsmanship

Warfare was deeply entwined in the ancient Celtic art, religion, lifestyle, and social structure. The Celts quickly acquired a warrior reputation among the other cultures in the ancient world. However, much of their barbaric reputation was attributed to them by the Romans, who intended to make the Celts look far scarier and uncivilized than they actually were. Celtic metalworkers used iron, bronze, and gold with tremendous skill, and many of their technological innovations found their way onto the battlefield. Some of the modern metalwork techniques hail from Celtic metalworking. However, when it came to war strategies, the Celtic warriors were less organized than they were portrayed to be by the Romans.

Celtic burials offer a cornucopia of information about the development of their warrior culture. The practice of burying prominent society members with objects related to their status (leaders and wealthier people) and warfare (in the case of warriors) originates from the Celts. Archeological findings have revealed that the Celtic warrior burials can be differentiated from other tombs in prehistoric cemeteries by their elaborate construction and the abundance of additional items they contain.

Celtic warriors were often buried with horse gear and weapons. The archeological findings also indicate that vehicles like carts, chariots, or wagons also found their way into Celtic warrior burial mounds. Sometimes, the buried objects were owned by the deceased in life. At other times, the interment resulted from local beliefs and traditions. For example, placing certain weapons (a sword, a helmet, or a spear) or personal possessions of chieftains had a religious significance for some Celtic tribes.

Across Europe, the Celts were known for their artistic ingenuity and have been credited with creating intricate stone carvings and delicate metal accessories. Creating panoply (armor) was one of the Celtic craftsman's strong suits. As evidenced by archeological findings and Roman writings about the Celts, the ancient Celtic warriors went to battle armed with shields, spears, and swords. Their shields were long and oval to protect vital body parts and often adorned with large bronze or iron bosses (studs in the middle of the shield). The swords, worn on the hip or side, were attached to an iron or bronze chain. The spears used by the Celts varied from lighter ones suitable for direct combat to heavier ones that doubled as lances. Early on, the Celtic armor was fashioned from fabric or leather – only to be replaced by chain mail shirts around the 4th century B.C.E. Chain mails featured tiny interlocking iron circles, which rendered them lighter, allowing the warriors far more freedom of movement. Shirts with broad shoulder straps emerged to help redistribute the chain mail shirt's weight even more. This also added extra protection to the shoulder and back.

Breastplates were also worn among the Celtic warriors in the 6th and 8th centuries B.C.E. There are also records of the Celts using helmets. Despite popular belief, early Celtic headpieces were only used during ceremonies. Instead of protection, they represented a status symbol. Fashioned from expensive and heavy materials like bronze, iron, gold, and coral, it's clear that they were too impractical to be worn during a battle. However, they were all the more suitable for making the wearer stand out in ceremonies. Since Celtic helmets became more practical in the later period, it's presumed that their use was transferred to the battlefield as well.

Celtic Art Symbolism

Celtic art is believed to hail from the much older Indo-European Iron Age. However, some parts of Celtic art can also be traced back to the neighboring nations like the Romans, Greeks, Etruscans, Scythians, and Thracians. Clothes and accessories were the most prominent testimony of Celtic art being featured in everyday life. By the end of the Iron Age, commoners wore long linen or wool trousers (depending on the season) with long-sleeved tunics made from a similar material. However, the wealthy people in society would sometimes have clothing made of silk adorned with intricate designs. In the wintertime, they wore cloaks secured with accessories featuring different symbols. Brooches and armlets were popular at all times of the year. The Celtic torc was probably one of their most prominent accessories, featuring a metal (typically gold) collar around the neck. These were used to identify high-ranking members of society.

The Celts created intricate art pieces in various mediums, from pottery and jewelry to animal figurines and ornate cauldrons. They mostly worked with locally sourced stone, iron, bronze, and gold for the main pieces. While the decorations were made from imported materials like glass, coral, and amber, the decoration depicts symbols that have to be attributed to Celtic traditions.

One of the most renowned Celtic symbols is the Triskele. It depicts three spirals creating a unique rotational symmetry. The triskele is commonly featured in Celtic art and traditions. It's also associated with contemporary Celtic or Pagan traditions. There are several versions of this symbol. For example, the three spirals can be pictured with three bent legs.

The Druids

The Druids were a class of highly educated people within ancient Celtic society. Their ranks included doctors, philosophers, poets, mathematicians, and spiritual leaders. Besides being an elite group, the Druids created a legacy based on the extensive knowledge they've collected over their lifetime. Just like Celtic culture, Druidism was also retained and evolved. Eventually, Druids became associated with magic, mysterious abilities, and deep spiritualism. The history of evolution in the Druidic society followed the development of the Celtic civilization.

Druids were considered an essential part of the Celtic community and were often sought out for their wisdom – to resolve different issues the tribe members or community faced. The word Druid can be traced back to the Latin and Gaulish words "*Druidae*" and "*Druides.*" The word can be broken down into two Celtic words, "*dru*" and "*wid,*" which translate as tree and wisdom, respectively. The word reflects the importance of trees in Celtic spiritualism and society. According to other sources, the word druid can also mean magician and sorcerer, a reference to the mystical powers Druids possessed according to the later Celtic societies.

The ancient Druids were classified into a structured hierarchical system based on rank and profession. Each class of Druids had a specific color associated with their status, which also symbolized their role in the Druid system. The eldest and wisest Druids had gold-colored robes. These were known as the *Arch-Druids* and often were approached when a leader had to make a decision that affected their entire community. Ordinary or general Druids wore white robes and usually acted as priests or teachers. Warrior Druids would wear red robes and were also known as sacrificers. Blue robes were worn by artistic Druids classified as bards. The new recruits wore brown or black robes. The different Druid classes had varied life patterns based on the natural cycle they were taught to follow. Among those patterns were following the lunar, solar, and seasonal cycles – and celebrating them with the appropriate events.

Celtic Folklore

Celtic mythology is a fascinating source of folkloric elements emanating from ancient Celtic cultures like the Irish, the Welsh, and the Gauls. Unfortunately, many Celtic myths were only recorded by Roman conquerors during Medieval times, which resulted in them being altered.

That said, it's known that the ancient Celts worshipped a much larger pantheon of deities than their successors. Depending on the location, these gods and goddesses often had different names and features. Some were widely honored by all Celts, while others were only regional deities celebrated in smaller communities.

The Celts' belief in many deities stemmed from the roles each of these gods played. However, the details of the Celtic polytheistic religion are debated because the Celts didn't record their religious practices. Much of the descriptions of these customs come, once again, from Roman literary sources.

Some of the deities of the Celtic pantheon include:
- **Aengus**, the god of love and poetry
- **Badb**, a war goddess
- **Brigid**, the goddess of fertility
- **Cernunnos**, the horned deity
- **Dagda**, the Celtic chief-turned deity
- **Lugh**, the god of justice
- **Morrigan**, another was a goddess/ an aspect of Badb

With some variations across different regions and tribes, components of the ancient Celtic culture included:
- The use of sacred groves, rivers, springs, and other natural sites for ceremonies and rituals involving the reverence of nature, the deities that rule spirits, and other entities.

- Frequent offerings dedicated to different deities, asking for blessings, protection, or healing powers. The offerings included sacrificed animals, weapons, and food items.
- A strong reverence for the afterlife – they often deposited valuables and everyday goods in the deceased's tombs.
- Religious ceremonies were often led by Druids and other highly distinguished tribe members.
- A firm belief in the protective powers of totems, taboos, and sacrifices, especially in times of need.

Chapter 2: Celtic Beliefs and Symbolism

Celtic symbolism can be defined as a set-up of signs and symbols used by the Celts to communicate their beliefs, culture, and spirituality. Besides representing a powerful relationship between signs and ideas, Celtic symbolism is also a unique representation of the Celts' connection to the natural world. From a historical perspective, Celtic symbolism can be traced back to the ancient Celts. Their rich mythology and folklore, and even beyond, to the roots that connect them to other pagan belief systems. Understanding the symbols in the context of Celtic spirituality and paganism can help you see who the ancient Celts were and how they lived their lives. And by looking into these symbols, you can deepen your connection to the natural world, tap into the wisdom of the Celtic tradition, and use it in your day-to-day life.

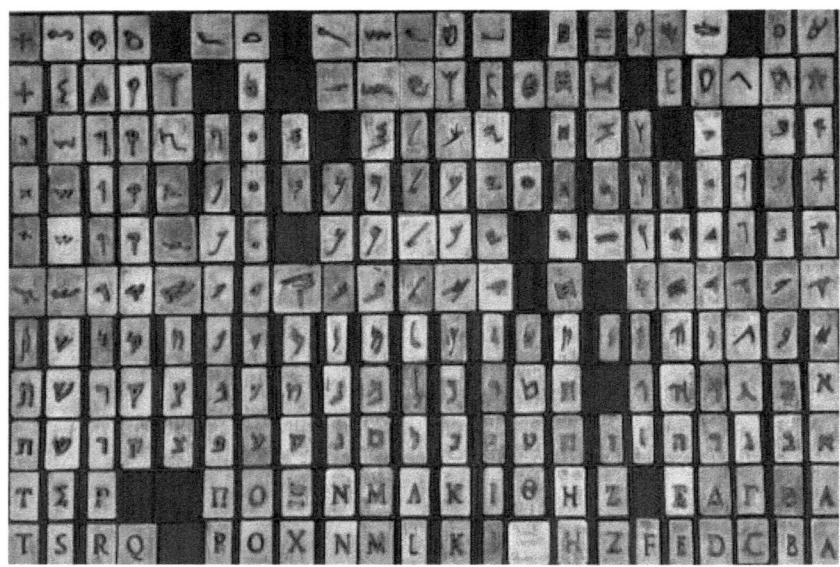

The Celts used symbols and gestures to communicate and spread their culture.
https://unsplash.com/photos/axYekjy6Kn4

The Celtic Pantheon

The polytheistic belief system of the Celts included reverence for a large number of deities. There are no written records of how these gods and goddesses were worshipped. However, archeological findings provide clues on the variations and commonalities in worship that existed across time and space and between the many ancient Celtic tribes. For example, there is evidence that the Celts often used natural sites like groves, springs, and clearings in elevated spaces to perform rituals and make offerings to their deities.

Nowadays, historians claim that the Celtic pantheon counts more than 400 deities. While some of these beings were at one point imagined as having human-like characteristics, most of them are considered supernatural entities that appear in their own unique form. Some deities worshipped by the Celts were similar to those venerated by other European belief systems. However, the Celts often made them their own by giving them different names while maintaining the same attributes, responsibilities, and powers. Other deities were entirely local – these often appear in the myths of tribes more isolated from the rest of the Celtic tribes and other religions in general. To further complicate the issue, the Celtic deities were given powers and associations that overlapped with those of other gods and goddesses in the Celtic pantheon. That said, these overlapping attributes are unique to the Celtic culture.

Fortunately, Celtic symbolism can also offer further clues about the role of Celtic deities in the cultures of their followers. Inscriptions used for rituals during worship and burial practices suggest that the deities had a powerful hold over people's lives. More often than not, venerating a particular divinity was necessary to maintain the tribe's well-being.

Many gods and goddesses were linked to natural places and phenomena like the sun, water, and lightning – indicating they provided sustenance, healing, and a means of survival. In the times of ancient Celts, finding food and ensuring a plentiful harvest was a well-known concern, and many deities were called upon to assist with hunting in general and even for particular animals like boars and stags and harvest. Others were associated with warfare, families, and tribes and were called upon for protection and guidance to defeat the enemy and preserve people's lives.

One of the most widely revered Celtic deities was Lugh (or Lugus, as he is known by the contemporary Celts), the god of the sun and light. According to many myths, he is very wise and all-seeing, making him one of the most influential Celtic deities. While he is rarely depicted in art, Lugh has several historic sites and modern-day places named after him. Cerunnos, on the other hand, is a Celtic deity often featured in Celtic symbolism and art. Known as the horned god, Cerunnos is depicted sitting on his magnificent throne, with horns or antlers on his head. His headpiece is a clear indication of his association with his animal nature.

Interestingly, several Celtic deities had triple roles or were viewed as three deities associated with the same natural aspect or facet of life. Some goddesses have names yet represent three different aspects of the same deity. For example, the Celtic pantheon has three mother goddesses depicting fertility, strength, and power. These goddesses were patrons of mothers, children, and Mother Nature. Likewise, other groups like fishermen, metalworkers, and bards have their own patron deities.

Besides having deities looking over certain aspects of nature, the Celts also found it fundamental to worship animals and plants as sacred beings with protective qualities. There is evidence of horses, boars, stags, bulls, and trees appearing as symbols of protection on Celtic armor, weapons, and everyday objects. Animals and plants were considered sacred in real life, too, and any offense to them was punishable – and not only in ancient times. For example, in Ireland, there are six sacred trees.

Celtic amulets offer intricate symbols of nature, making them perfect for the protection of the living and the deceased (as they journey to the Otherworld). Amulets were found in several burial mounds, indicating that those in the burial site had to be protected in the spiritual realm. The most widespread Celtic protective symbols are wheels, shoes, shields, and axes.

Cosmology and Sacred Sites

Much like in its Norse counterpart, the world has three parts in Celtic cosmology – the Sky (Heaven), the Earth, and the Otherworld. At the core of the world is the World Tree, or the Tree of Life, as it is known by the Celts. The tree's highest branches reach Heaven, while its roots go deep into the Otherworld. The latter is surrounded by water, from which the tree gains sustenance. Because of this, the Celts consider bodies of water as gates to the Otherworld. Not only are many burial mounds located near water, but they are also deeply revered worship sites.

The Celts believed springs host supernatural beings like fairies, nymphs, and spirits. The reverence for the springs and its inhabitants is mirrored by archaeological finds associated with the Celts. There are numerous sites where archeologists unearthed stones, animal bones, and Celtic artifacts near springs. Some of these springs are still believed to have curative powers associated with a particular deity. According to legends, lakes were the best places to contact the spirits, gods, and goddesses of the Otherworld. From the archeological findings in several lakes, it can be deduced that people offered sacrifices to the spirits here. There are entire hordes of items people have thrown into lakes in hopes of summoning the spirits. Rivers in places where the ancient Celts lived are often named after Celtic deities associated with powers like protection, healing, and whatever else the Celts required to navigate their lives. Sometimes warriors offered their shields to the gods to honor or appease them because some of the Celtic deities had a volatile nature.

Boglands also have holy aspects, according to the Celts. They are typically associated with protection and supernatural beings like fairies and were often used for rituals and offerings. Some archeological evidence suggests that bogs also served as a final resting place for bards,

Druids, and those who delved into magic and other mysterious arts.

Besides consecrated springs, rivers, and bogs, the Celts had other natural sites they considered sacred. Mountains, hilltops, and groves of trees often served as ritual sites. According to oral tradition, the Druids found it particularly conducive to use these sights to gather wisdom and power. Oak is one of the trees the Celts considered sacred. Besides providing shade for people to assemble during rites and ceremonies, the oak trees are also attributed with liminal powers. It represented a connection between this realm and all the other realms – evidenced by the fact that the oak tree is often used to symbolize the Tree of Life in Celtic art.

Some sacred places connected to the earth were entirely natural, while others were man-made. There are several sites where archeologists found stones and bowls buried in the ground. The latter was likely for collecting offerings and performing animal sacrifices and divinations. Most were found in the open countryside, in clearings, or surrounded by wood. The artificial sacred sites also included stone circles, gates, and similar monuments. In some places, animal bones inside the stones offer evidence that animal sacrifices were made to protect the site and those using it from malicious spiritual influences. The sacred groves used by the Druids had similar aspects, as they were also man-made and had protective and power-enhancing elements.

Certain sacred places in connection to the Earth also offered a link to the sky. These were higher monuments, either natural, like mountaintops, or man-made. The latter was characteristic of later periods when the Celts began to build temples mimicking other cultures' spiritual and religious traditions. In a natural setting, the man-made natural monuments had only a few artificial elements. For example, people would make an indentation in a natural rock sitting in a clearing and use it for rituals, divination, and other purposes. In Scotland and Ireland, there are several of these sites where Celtic kings are believed to have proclaimed their kingship or addressed people before a battle or other critical event in their lives.

While later on, the Celts began to prepare sacred sites in more urban settings, these places still had a powerful link to nature. Purpose-built monuments on the earth symbolize people's connection to the earth. Whereas shrines and temples were erected to empower their connection to the deities. Megalithic structures erected by earlier civilizations also inspired the Celts to create their own religious sites by transforming the older structure based on their needs. Celtic sacred sites with a rectangular or square clearing surrounded by artificial channels dug into the earth were revealed in Bohemia, France, and southern Germany. The channels represented the perimeter of the site. Some even featured a gate on the east. Historians hypothesize that the bare space in the middle was once filled with strategically placed wooden poles the Celts used to record monumental events. They probably adorned the poles with symbols depicting natural phenomena, people's names and occupations, wars, and more. Others think that some wooden poles acted as supporting beams for temples. Some poles had deep shafts carved into them for votive offerings. Archeological findings from the 2nd and 1st centuries B.C.E. indicate that the Celts also used items made with pottery and metalwork in sacrificial sites. These items had symbols associated with deities, spirits, and the natural world.

The oldest Celtic stone temples were built in the 4th century B.C.E. These featured spacious doorways adorned with early Celtic symbols. Their roof was often made of intertwining branches (referencing the Celtic reverence toward the trees) held together with clay and lime. The Celtic belief about the soul residing in the head was also showcased with the ornate masks Celts used to decorate their ancient temples. After being conquered by the Romans, Celts shifted to erecting temples featuring classical Roman architectural elements. However, they found a way to give homage to the ancient gods with featureless adornments covered in metal torcs. Before that, it was rare for the Celts to depict deities through stone monuments. If they did, these were simple standing stone pillars or carvings made into domes adorned with the representations of the head (and, through it, the soul) and nature. The latter was depicted via symbols of plants, trees, and other vegetal designs.

Symbolism in Rituals and Offerings

Celtic rituals are often held to honor nature, the spirits and the afterlife, and the deities. Rites that follow the schedule based on nature's cycles, the Moon's phases, and other heavenly bodies offer a powerful connection to these elements. Each had a cyclical nature, which the Celts associated with the cycle of life.

Incantations and prayers were recited to the deities, and votive offerings were made to them since ancient times. Sometimes, the symbolism of the deity worship was tied to other beliefs. For example, in Scotland and Ireland, there are several sites where places of worship and ritual were erected near burial mounds. In these places, several mounds represent the graves of important individuals whose power could have been used to empower rituals and ceremonies. These places still have visitors that leave small offerings in the hope of obtaining empowerment, guidance, or recovery from ailments.

Interestingly enough, unlike the objects found in the burial grounds, the items in the worship sites appeared to be broken. It is believed that this was the Celt's way of denouncing the object and stating that it now belonged to the god, goddess, or spirit they offered it to.

While Roman and other literary sources suggest that human sacrifice was practiced among the ancient Celts, there is little evidence of whether this was true or simply Rome's way of making the Celts look more barbaric. Animal sacrifices were common, but even these rituals have been discarded over the centuries. Whether ancestors were buried or burned, contemporary Celtic pagans only offered animal parts they would discard after preparing the rest for a meal.

Besides protection, ancient Celts also used animal sacrifices for divination. Different animal parts were associated with district aspects of life, and based on this, they offered clues about the future events in these aspects.

A unique form of offering was the burial of items. They were often buried in shallow ground after being offered precious goods for a cause. Several objects (like torcs, coins, and necklaces) were tied together or covered with a piece of fabric before being deposited into the ground. Items were often offered and buried on the same site (not in the same pit but others nearby) over many years. The number of items found in these places implies that the area was considered sacred. Despite initially viewing them as safety deposits, historians now agree they were part of an ancient Celtic ritual. The sites were likely associated with a deity, a protective or healing aspect of nature, or represented a liminal space.

When it comes to the unique Celtic burial mounds, these were tied to the Celts' deep reverence towards the afterlife. Celtic pagan traditions affirm that when a person dies in this world, their soul travels to the Otherworld. However, when one person dies, another is born, and their soul emerges to the earth. Sometimes, those who journeyed to the Otherworld stay there to act as spiritual guides and protectors, particularly during the liminal periods. By burying their dead in natural sites, the ancient Celts symbolically gave them back to the earth where they came from. The items buried with them helped grant a safe journey and gain the assistance of the gods of the Otherworld.

Other Prominent Symbolism in Celtic Culture

Besides the movement of the moon, sun, and other heavenly bodies, ancient Celtic cosmology revolved around symbolism, including spirals and wheels. Both of these are linked to the never-ending cycle of life. The seasons turned each year like points on a giant wheel – hence many Celtic pagans followed and still followed a calendar called the Wheel of the Year.

The symbolism of the stars is tied to the belief in the North Star, the axis of the sky – which also represented the gates of the heavens. According to Celtic mythology, as the stars moved around this axis, they formed a spiral path.

The continuous spirals are also tied to the Celtic belief that when one cycle ends, another commences. The seemingly endless expansion of the spiral might also denote that wisdom can be grown too. Triplicate symbols are said to be attributed to divine empowerment.

Since the ancient Celts based their calendar on the moon's cycles, their year had 13 months. Twelve are similar to the months in modern calendars, while the 13th has only three days and only acted as a guide for those preparing for the coming year. Additionally, each month has a sacred Ogham tree linked to it.

Each of the four seasons was celebrated with a specific holiday, marking a momentous occasion in people's lives. Samhain, which marks the beginning of the winter and the cessation of hunting and harvesting, and Beltane, the festival that welcomes the summer and the beginning of true life in nature, are both traditionally celebrated with fire. During these periods, the veil between the worlds becomes thinner, allowing spirits from the Otherworld to come to and fro, sending and carrying messages. Imbolc and Lughnasadh are two other fire festivals observing events like Solstices and Equinoxes. Several ritual sites are built in a way that they align with these points on the Wheel of the Year.

Around the festivals, the Celts were even more fascinated by the liminal spaces, like doorways and shorelines, and considered them places of empowerment. They would often gather on the shore where they could make a connection between the solid, material world and the fluid spiritual world. The festivals also provide a fantastic opportunity for the Celts to approach their deities and ancestors.

Tree of Life

This symbol is frequently featured in art and used widely in Celtic rituals, ceremonies, or ways of life in general. Nowadays, you can see it in jewelry, talismans, and even tattoos. However, its significance goes much deeper than being an aesthetically pleasing design. The Tree of Life represented a connection to the natural world for thousands of years. Given that trees are always a vital source of food, shelter, firewood, and medicine for humanity, it's easy to see why a tree may have a significant symbolism in the Celtic culture.

It's believed that the Druids played a fundamental role in giving trees spiritual significance. Besides using them for rituals and worship, they also knew that trees (especially the oak) were a great place to look for mistletoe – a tree with spiritually empowering effects.

After arriving on new territory, ancient Celtic tribes often settled around a tree (like an oak), which acted as a central point for community activities like rituals and ceremonies. The Celts believed that forming the settlement around the tree granted the community wisdom, strength, and longevity. If you are wondering why oaks were the most common trees used for this purpose, the answer lies in their longevity. The lifespan of an Oak tree can reach up to several hundred years.

Other trees used as focal points or places of worship near a community were yews – which live even longer, for thousands of years. To this day, the Celts also believe that given that roots of the trees extend deep into the ground, this symbolizes the connection between the Tree of Life and the Otherworld. They use trees to connect with their ancestors.

Chapter 3: A-Z of Celtic Symbols

This chapter delves into the interpretations and spiritual meanings of various symbols found in Celtic mythology, folklore, and spirituality.

Ailm

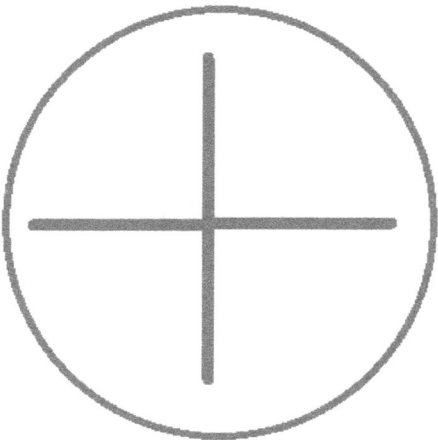

Ailm is a symbol of flexibility and maturity.

This symbol comes from the first letter of Ogham, believed to have been the earliest form of written communication in Celtic Ireland. It is a symbol of an evergreen conifer, known as silver fir. People at the time referred to a particular group of trees as the Ogham because they thought these conifers had an indispensable amount of wisdom to share. In Celtic mythology, evergreens have powerful healing powers and can revitalize the human soul. Ailms are symbols of flexibility, rehabilitation, maturity, strength, resilience, and inner power.

Awen represents the virtues of truth, love, and wisdom.
https://commons.wikimedia.org/wiki/File:Awen_symbol_final.svg

The Awen symbol is also referred to as the "Three Rays of Light" because it's shown as three circles, each representing sources or centers of light, with a ray extending from each. A renowned Welsh poet was the first to mention this neo-Druid symbol during the 18th century. Researchers, however, suggest that the invention of the Awen goes back further.

The term "Awen" translates to "essence" or "inspiration," which is why there are various interpretations of what the symbol stands for. Some practitioners believe that the three rays are representative of the essence of life; air, sea, and earth. Others suggest they symbolize the essence of humans or mind, body, and spirit. According to some interpretations, the three rays are symbols of the most important virtues of truth, love, and wisdom.

Truthfulness, compassion, and understanding are the three cornerstones of awakening and are believed to be represented by the three rays. Many people think that reinvigoration and the state of being present and conscious come from inspiration. Awakening, however, goes hand-in-hand with the truth. You can't seek the truth if you're not awake.

Simpler interpretations of the symbol suggest that the Awen represents the ability of opposite forces to exist harmoniously in the universe. Masculine and feminine energies are depicted as the left and right rays, while the middle ray symbolizes the harmony and balance maintained between both energies.

Beltane

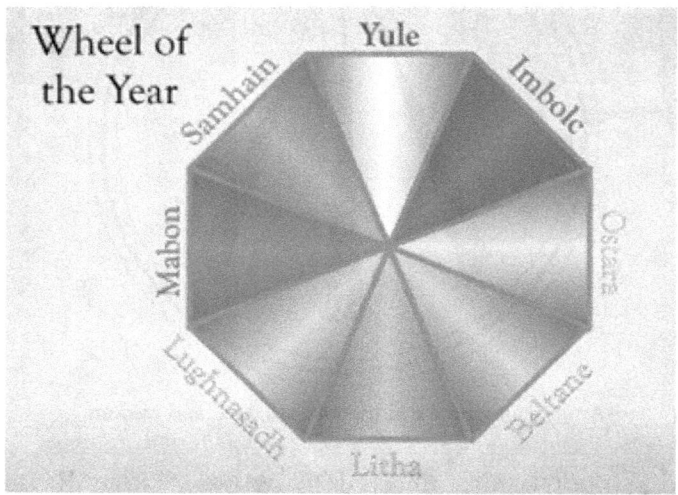

The wheel of the year.
Imbolc.cerddwr, CC BY-SA 3.0 <https://creativecommons.org/licenses/by-sa/3.0>, via Wikimedia Commons: https://commons.wikimedia.org/wiki/File:Wheel_of_the_year.png

The Wheel of the Year is a Celtic calendar that revolves around eight seasonal festivals: Imbolc, Ostara, Beltane, Litha, Lughnasa, Mabon, Samhain, and Yule. Each of the eight sabbats, or festivals, has its own symbol. Beltane is celebrated on May 1st to welcome summer, and people pray to the deities for abundance in crops and good weather. This celebration falls right between the spring equinox and the summer solstice.

Brigid's Cross

This symbol is among the oldest Celtic Irish emblems and can be traced to the goddess Brigid in the Celtic myth Tuatha de Danaan. Many suggest this deity was later transfigured into the Christian saint of Kildare after the religion made its way into Ireland. Practitioners believe they can invoke the saint's or goddess' protective energies if they hang this symbol on their doors or in the corridors.

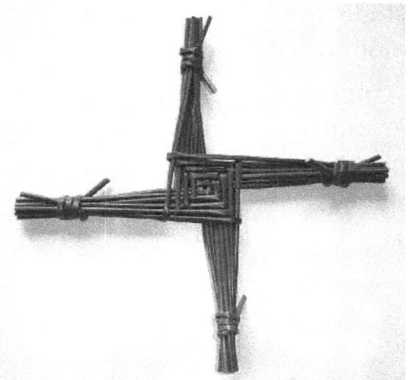

A Brigid's Cross is made out of straws and rushes.
Culnacreann, CC BY 3.0 <https://creativecommons.org/licenses/by/3.0>, via Wikimedia Commons: https://commons.wikimedia.org/wiki/File:Saint_Brigid%27s_cross.jpg

Straw and rushes are conventionally used to weave the cross on the Sabbat Imbolc, which is the day that celebrates the goddess Brigid. According to lore, this symbol was initially gifted to her father on his deathbed. The goddess' father knew that the cross was a holy symbol, which is why he felt the need to be baptized and die in purity.

Bowen Knot

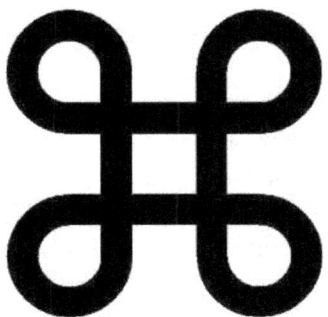

The loops in a Bowen knot symbolize true love, loyalty, and flowing water.
Jpbowen at the English-language Wikipedia, CC BY-SA 3.0 <http://creativecommons.org/licenses/by-sa/3.0/>, via Wikimedia Commons: https://commons.wikimedia.org/wiki/File:Bowen_knot.jpg

Celtic knots are patterns of loops and knots that have symbolic meanings. That they have neither a beginning nor an end symbolizes the infinite nature of life. Celtic knots can be traced back to the 8th century and have been used by practitioners to decorate their spaces and bring certain energies into their lives. Each Celtic pattern or knot symbolizes different virtues or emotions and has unique interpretations.

The Bowen knot comes in different forms. The two most common are a square with four outward-pointing loops at each corner or a cross with four pointy loops at each end. These loops symbolize true love, loyalty, and flowing water.

Celtic Spiral

Spirals are emblems of spiritual growth and development.
https://commons.wikimedia.org/wiki/File:Triskele-Symbol-spiral-five-thirds-turns.svg

According to Celtic mythology, spirals are emblems of spiritual growth and development. Spirals are also symbols of energy constantly emitted from human bodies and their surroundings. They also represent space and the infinite nature of the universe. The Celtic spiral suggests that humans are always in a state of evolution and experiencing balance among their minds, bodies, and spirits.

They are often used to decorate spaces and are depicted in various forms to convey certain meanings. A single spiral that rotates counterclockwise represents human growth and development throughout life. A single spiral that rotates clockwise is representative of water and movement.

Double spirals symbolize the dual nature of all existence, representing the balance between two contrasting forces. Wet and dry, feminine and masculine, and night and day, for example, can all be represented by double spirals. The duality of nature is needed to maintain balance and harmony. A double spiral which is centered is an emblem of harmony and the moon. A combined double spiral symbolizes different directions.

Cernunnos

Cernunnos symbol.
Otourly, CC BY-SA 3.0 <https://creativecommons.org/licenses/by-sa/3.0>, via Wikimedia Commons: https://commons.wikimedia.org/wiki/File:Horned-God-Symbol.svg

The ancient Celts considered Cernunnos one of the most important deities in the pantheon, which is why his symbol remains one of the most popular. He is the god of life, animal, fertility, and wild animals. He is also the underworld deity and is associated with the natural cycle of death and rebirth. Cernunnos is often illustrated sitting cross-legged with antlers on his head, and his symbol is a circle with an upward-facing crescent, symbolizing a horned head.

Circular Knots

Circular knots can come in this pattern.
https://commons.wikimedia.org/wiki/File:Trefoil-triquetra-circular-arcs-around-triangle_(solid).svg

Circular knots come in various patterns and sizes, depending on the energy the user wishes to bring into their life. Circular knots mainly symbolize inner life, the infinite nature of life, the cycle of life, and the sun.

Cross of Triquetras

The Cross of Triquetras is also referred to as the Carolingian Cross.
Madboy74, CC BY-SA 4.0 <https://creativecommons.org/licenses/by-sa/4.0>, via Wikimedia Commons: https://commons.wikimedia.org/wiki/File:Coa_Illustration_Cross_Carolingian.svg

The Cross of Triquetras, also known as the Carolingian Cross, symbolizes motherhood, virginity, purity, and wisdom. These virtues are considered the three aspects of the goddess. This Celtic symbol is also associated with the rotation of the sun and its position in the sky (sunset, sunrise, zenith, etc.). Some historical accounts suggest that this symbol was also used as an emblem for the male trinity.

Dara Celtic Knot

The Dara knot takes the shape of an oak tree's roots.

The term "*Dara*" is derived from an ancient Celtic word that means "oak." This is why the symbol takes the intricate shape of an old oak tree's roots. Like all the other Celtic knots, the Dara knot has neither a beginning nor an end. Oak trees were sacred to the Celts because they were associated with their deities and played significant roles in ancient Celtic legends. They were also places of worship and were believed to be gateways to the otherworld. Oak trees were believed to be sources of knowledge and wisdom, which is why people often turned to them for guidance. The oak tree is a source of nourishment and inner strength, and wisdom.

Druid Sigil

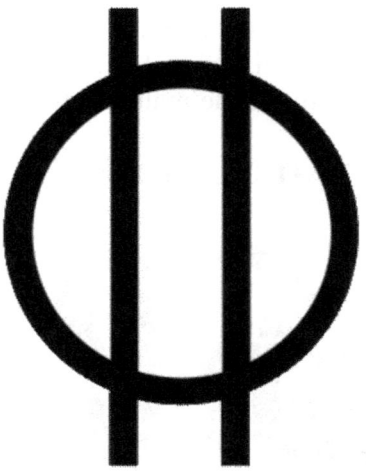

The Druid Sigil.
Shii (Communications Officer, Reformed Druids of Carleton College), CC0, via Wikimedia Commons: https://commons.wikimedia.org/wiki/File:Reformed_Druids.svg

A Druid Sigil takes the shape of a circle and has two lines that look like tree branches inside. Sigils are commonly used in ritual magic and symbolize fertility, reproduction, and Mother Nature.

Eostre

Eostre, also known as Ostara, is celebrated on the spring equinox, usually on March 20th in the northern hemisphere. Practitioners celebrate Ostara because it symbolizes the balance between two extreme weathers (summer and winter) and light and dark because the day is equally split between daytime and nighttime during the equinox. This festival is considered the predecessor of modern-day Easter.

Eternity Knot

The eternity knot is important in many religions and cultures.
AnonMoos (initial SVG conversion of PostScript source by AnonMoos was done by Indolences), Public domain, via Wikimedia Commons: https://commons.wikimedia.org/wiki/File:Triquetra-circle-interlaced.svg

The eternal knot is an important symbol in many religions and cultures around the world, including Buddhism, Jainism, Hinduism, Tibet, Buryatia, and Mongolia. The Celtic eternity knot looks unique and is generally the most popular. The knot has a beautiful design symbolizes eternity, love, and romantic and non-romantic relationships.

Five-Fold Symbol

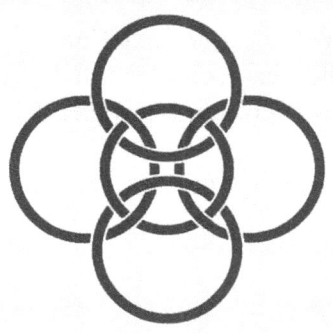

The five-fold symbol represents spirituality and faith.

While this is among the lesser-known Celtic emblems, the five-fold symbol is one of the most significant. The five interwoven circles of the emblem symbolize the five traditional Celtic basic elements of the universe. The emblem also represents spirituality, God, faith, and heaven, or the four cardinal directions. The fifth ring, in either case, symbolizes harmony, balance, or the universe.

Imbolc

Imbolc, which is also referred to as St. Brigid's Day, takes place on February 1st. This festival marks the beginning of spring and is right between the Winter solstice and the spring equinox. Practitioners celebrate Imbolc because this is when light or sunshine returns.

Litha

This sabbat is celebrated between the 20th and 23rd of June, marking midsummer or the summer solstice in the northern hemisphere. Litha is also the longest day of the year and is celebrated for its agricultural fertility and abundance.

Lughnasadh

This is a Gaelic festival that takes place on August 1st, marking the start of the harvest season. This festival is named after the Celtic deity Lughnasadh, the deity of harvest, agriculture, and livestock, and it is celebrated in his honor.

Mabon

Mabon is celebrated on the Autumnal Equinox between the 21st and 24th of September. Like Eostre, this holiday celebrates balance and harmony in the universe. This day is perfectly split between day and night.

Quaternary Celtic Knot

Quaternary knots protect users from negative energy.
https://cdn4.vectorstock.com/i/1000x1000/76/93/quaternary-celtic-knot-symbol-choosing-the-right-vector-40797693.jpg

Knots with four loops weren't very common among ancient Celts because they preferred using circular knots or ones with three loops. Quaternary knots, however, are still very popular because they help protect their users from negative energy. This knot is a symbol of groundedness and support. It offers a sense of peace, confidence, and stability.

Samhain

This sabbat is celebrated on November 1st, marking the start of winter and the end of the harvesting season. As Eostre is the predecessor of Easter, Samhain is believed to be the forerunner of Halloween. This holiday is connected to the ancestors and the world of the dead.

The Bird

Birds were believed to be the messengers of the gods.
https://unsplash.com/photos/vUNQaTiZeOo?utm_source=unsplash&utm_medium=referral&utm_content=creditShareLink

Animals played a significant role in the ancient Celtic life. Celts used to inscribe symbols of the animals on their amulets and ornaments to bring specific energy and meanings into their lives. They used images of birds to symbolize freedom and bridge the gap between Earth and the heavens. Birds were believed to be the messengers of the gods.

The Boar

Boards represent both stubbornness and the kindness of women.
https://unsplash.com/photos/oSaq0J4zGE0?utm_source=unsplash&utm_medium=referral&utm_content=creditShareLink

This animal had two distinct meanings in the ancient Celtic world. It stood for stubbornness, persistence, and strength of warriors. It was also associated with the hospitality and kindness of women. People enjoyed its meat as a delicacy.

The Bull

The Celts considered bulls sacred.
https://unsplash.com/photos/oSaq0J4zGE0?utm_source=unsplash&utm_medium=referral&utm_content=creditShareLink

Depictions of bulls were used to decorate nearly every ancient Celtic home. This animal was considered sacred and was venerated by all. The bull is thought to be a symbol of prosperity and fertility, which is why people wanted to bring its energy into their homes.

The Cauldron

The Cauldron was a symbol of well-being.
https://www.pexels.com/photo/smoke-coming-from-iron-cauldron-16010709/

The Cauldron symbolized well-being and was associated with feasting and matters of the dead. Ancient Celts incorporated large cauldrons into their funerary rites and believed that they were vessels that transported the dead to the otherworld. The Cauldron was also viewed as a symbol of rebirth and abundance. Some featured a cauldron that could feed hundreds of soldiers and revive dead warriors.

The Celtic Cross

The Celtic Cross represents the elements and directions.
https://commons.wikimedia.org/wiki/File:Celtic_cross.svg

This widespread Gaelic symbol incorporates a circle with a cross in the center. This emblem is representative of the elements and the directions. This symbol's sense of continuity symbolizes the eternal development of humans. Practitioners believed that carrying this symbol around would give them knowledge and guidance, and protect them from unwanted forces, as it combines the Christian symbol of the cross and the Celtic symbol of the sun.

The Claddagh Ring

The Claddagh ring is a symbol of marriage and love.
*Miguel Mendez from Malahide, Ireland, CC BY 2.0
<https://creativecommons.org/licenses/by/2.0>, via Wikimedia Commons:
https://commons.wikimedia.org/wiki/File:Claddagh_ring_(7061237901).jpg*

This ring is named after the island on which it was created. The Claddagh ring is a Celtic symbol of marriage, love, and romantic and non-romantic relationship. The ring comprises a heart, which resembles love, and a crown on top of it, which is an emblem of loyalty. Wearing the heart on one's finger symbolizes protection, guidance, and support.

The Deer

Deers are associated with the Tree of Life.
https://unsplash.com/photos/FGkNt8tO04I?utm_source=unsplash&utm_medium=referral&utm_content=creditShareLink

The deer is associated with the Tree of Life because it represents the unity of the universe. The animal is a symbol of strength, and its horns, characterized by their ability to regrow, signify the power of nature. Ancient Celts drew on the energy of this animal to grow and revitalize their spirituality.

The Green Man

The Green Man is a symbol of rebirth.
Rosser1954, CC BY-SA 4.0 <https://creativecommons.org/licenses/by-sa/4.0>, via Wikimedia Commons: https://commons.wikimedia.org/wiki/File:Green_Man_water_feature.jpg

The Green Man is a symbol of rebirth and is associated with spring. Some ancient Celts believed that this figure was the protector of the forest. According to some historical accounts, this symbol was eminent in several legends across different cultures. The Green Man was particularly important to Celtic tradition because they believed that nature was sacred, were largely concerned about the fertility of their lands, and viewed abundant harvest as a sign of prosperity.

The Sailor's Knot

The sailor's knot symbolizes the undying nature of true love.

The strong and intricate weaving of the sailor's knot symbolizes true love's perseverance and undying nature, regardless of how far away loved ones are. This symbol shows that true love holds out against rough waves and storms, representing all the obstacles that come with life. Sailors used to give these symbols in the form of amulets to their wives before they sailed off to remind them of their undying love. Sailors also kept the Sailor's Knot with them because they thought it had protective energies and attracted food fortune. They believed that carrying it around would keep the weather stable and protect and guide them throughout their journey.

The Shamrock

The shamrock was considered protection from negative energy.
https://unsplash.com/photos/NumcxeDrWUQ?utm_source=unsplash&utm_medium=referral&utm_content=creditShareLink

This is the most popular Irish symbol to this day. Celtic Lore suggests that St. Patrick explained the concept of the Trinity by pulling the shamrock from the earth. The Celts used this symbol to protect themselves from the evil eye, malice, and negative energies. It was also used to attract prosperity and good fortune.

The Tree of Life

This symbol looks like an encircled tree with hands reaching upward for branches. The roots are shaded and connected to the hands. This symbol is representative of the harmony and unity between the terrestrial, the underground, and the heavens. Celts believed trees were sacred beings and served as portals to the spirits, the heavens, and the ancestors.

Triquetra

Triquetra symbolizes the nature of life.
original raster image and vector PostScript source code by AnonMoos, initial vectorization by Erin Silversmith, Public domain, via Wikimedia Commons:
https://commons.wikimedia.org/wiki/File:Triquetra-Double.svg

Ancient Celts believed that important things came in threes, which is why the Triquetra is considered one of the most important Celtic symbols. It comprises endless loops that symbolize the nature of life, beginning from birth to rebirth. The Triquetra is also associated with the Holy Trinity in Christianity.

Triskeles

This symbol represents the unity of the three elements of fire, earth, and water. It is formed of three spirals and is believed to be the oldest symbol of spirituality. Triskeles are symbols of the cycle of life or birth, death, and the rebirth that follows. It is also associated with the harmony between the mental, physical, and spiritual aspects of the self. The symbol communicates the message that all that is important in the world come in sets of three.

Wheel of Taranis

The Wheel of Taranis symbolizes the wheel of a ship.
Madboy74, CC BY-SA 4.0 <https://creativecommons.org/licenses/by-sa/4.0>, via Wikimedia Commons: https://commons.wikimedia.org/wiki/File:Coa_Illustration_Taranis_Wheel.svg

This symbol represents the wheel of a ship and is associated with the deities, the basic elements, the sun, and the sky. It is named after the Celtic god of thunder, Taranis. The deity is often depicted holding a wheel in one hand and a lightning bolt in the other.

Yule

Yule is celebrated between December 21st and January 1st, marking the winter solstice - the midpoint of winter. Practitioners anticipate the New Sun and the positivity and abundance it would bring to Earth.

Chapter 4: The Celtic Tree Calendar

Many ancient cultures were fascinated with astrology. They were curious to find how the stars' movements or the sun's positions could influence someone's personality and future. The ancient Celts were no different and had a huge interest in Zodiac signs. However, they had their own interpretation of astrology.

Unlike the Gregorian calendar, the Celtic tree system was based on the lunar cycle. Ancient humans used the Moon as a method to tell time and determine the days, weeks, and months. The Celts went through various experiments and rituals to understand how the lunar cycle worked until they developed their own unique system.

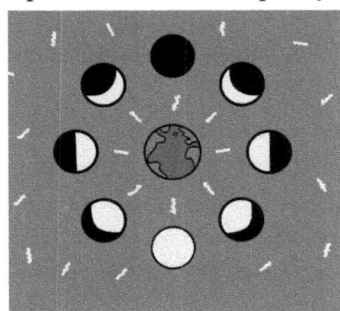

The Celts based their tree system on the lunar cycle.
Symbols illustrated by Jasmina El Bouamraoui and Karabo Poppy Moletsane, CC0, via Wikimedia Commons:
https://commons.wikimedia.org/wiki/File:Wikipedia20_background_Lunar_cycle.jpg

The calendar is divided into thirteen months, and each is linked to a tree associated with Celtic mythology and an Ogham alphabet (the ancient Irish alphabet that will be discussed in detail in the next chapter). These sacred trees are associated with magic, healing, elements, and deities.

This chapter covers the Celtic tree calendar and its origin and will provide detailed information about its zodiac signs.

The History and Mythology of the Celtic Tree Calendar

There have been many disagreements among scholars about the origin of the Celtic tree calendar. Some believe that it wasn't the ancient Celts who invented it but author and poet Robert Graves, a student of Irish and Celtic mythology. He created this system in 1948, making it a modern invention. He was influenced by the tree calendar that the Druids designed centuries ago.

Graves used the ancient "Song of Amergin" to create his system. The Song of Amergin is one of the oldest poems in the world. However, it is shrouded with mystery since no one knows who wrote it or when and where it was written. Graves believed the song was written in 1268 BC in the British Isles. He translated it and adapted the fifteen consonants of the ancient Ogham alphabet to thirteen letters to correspond with the thirteen lunar cycles that take place each year. Graves divided the calendar into thirteen months with twenty-eight days each and added an extra day to make the year 365 days.

The belief that Graves was the one who created the Celtic tree calendar is common among many scholars because no evidence suggests the Celts ever used this system.

Graves introduced the calendar in his book "The White Goddess," which focused on Middle Eastern, European, Irish, and British mythology. Since not much is known about the ancient Druids or the Celts, Graves was inspired by the works of Irish historian Ruaidhrí Ó Flaithbheartaigh. Ruaidhrí covered the history of Ireland, including its legends, myths, and the Ogham alphabet, in his books.

Whether all credit goes to Robert Graves or not, he wouldn't have been able to develop his system without the Druids laying the groundwork for him. He also based his work on Celtic folklore and mythology and combined it with modern discoveries and beliefs to create this brilliant calendar.

While other scholars agree that the Druids created this system, some modern Celtic pagans believe that the tree calendar existed before the Druids rose to power and became the most influential religious group among the Celts. Many scholars are inclined to believe that the tree system existed before the Druids, but they were the ones who improved on it and discovered the magical properties of each sacred tree.

Simply put: the system that existed before the Druids were the foundation they based their work on to create the Celtic tree calendar - still used today.

The sacred trees associated with the thirteen months have an interesting mythology behind them. The Druids believed that all mankind was the descendants of trees. Each one also symbolizes a Celtic god or goddess and has its own meaning and characteristics that influence the people born under its month. This resembles the concept of Zodiac signs that believe that the sun's position on the day you were born impacts your personality.

The Celtic Tree Zodiac

The Celtic tree zodiac is a system of astrology based on the ancient Celtic reverence for trees. The trees were considered sacred, believed to hold wisdom and power, and associated with particular qualities and characteristics. Each tree has its ruling planet, animal, gemstone, color, Ogham letter, and more. This zodiac system is more complex than Western and Chinese astrology because the Druids spent years studying trees. The ancient Celts predicted the future by listening to the leaves as they whispered their secrets to them. They also used the Ogham alphabet and the lunar cycles to determine people's characteristics.

The Tree Calendar and the Natural World

Nature has always been fascinating and piqued the interest of all poets and authors. Many stories and poems take place around nature, especially in the woods hence the terms magical or enchanted forest. Before the invention of medicine, plants, and herbs provided a remedy to all ailments, whether physical or mental.

Trees are the most majestic part of nature, they are powerful, unique, and old, and life would be impossible without them.

The ancient and Neo-Druids revere trees and would hold their ceremonies and meditate under them. The word "Druid" also means "the knowledge of the oak." They considered trees to be living beings capable of experiencing various emotions and connecting the Earth to the Heavens.

The Druids chose to associate their calendar with trees because they believed nature to be sacred. Trees also change colors during the seasons, making them the perfect representation of the cycle of nature and the changing seasons.

The tree calendar determines the festivals the ancient and neo-pagans celebrate to mark the beginning of each season. For instance, the Samhain festival celebrates the beginning of winter, and Ostara marks the beginning of spring. These festivals will be discussed in detail in the coming chapter.

Now that you understand the history and mythology behind the Celtic tree calendar, the second part of the chapter will focus on the thirteen sacred trees and what they represent.

Birch Moon (December 24 – January 20)

Elements
Air and water.
Seasons
Spring and fall.
Ruling Planet
Venus.
Color
White.
Gemstone
Crystal.
Animals
White stag and golden eagle.
Ogham Letter
Beith (B).
Symbolism
Regeneration, new beginnings, growth, and rebirth.

Correspondence

Capricorn.

Mythology

In Celtic mythology, the Birch tree symbolizes love. Ancient Celts placed their branches over newborns' cribs to protect them from harm and evil spirits.

Deity

Eostre, the goddess of spring.

Zodiac

People born under the birch tree are driven, goal-oriented, and ambitious. They are constantly working on developing themselves in various areas of their lives. Since these individuals are born during the darkest time of the year, they constantly look for the light in themselves and others. They are capable of finding beauty wherever they go. They are charming individuals who are always smiling and patient with others. Yet, they can be strong and tough leaders.

Rowan Moon (January 21 – February 17)

Element

Fire.

Seasons

Spring and fall.

Ruling Planet

The Sun.

Color

Gray.

Gemstone

Peridot.

Animal

Dragon.

Ogham Letter

Luis (L).

Symbolism

Connection, protection, and courage.

Correspondences
Pisces and Aquarius.
Mythology
The Celts associated this tree with success, power, and personal growth. They used to carve a charm on its twig and wear it for protection. Some cultures planted this tree in graveyards so the spirits of the dead wouldn't linger in the world of the living but would cross to the other side.
Deity
Brighid, the goddess of home and fertility.
Zodiac
People born under this sign are unique individuals. They have a vision and goals they work hard to achieve. Although they may seem cool and aloof on the outside, they are extremely passionate and energetic on the inside. They often have creative ideas and a wide imagination. People can find them intimidating because they can have a tough exterior. However, they are kind and caring individuals who are supportive of others.

Ash Moon (February 18 – March 17)
Elements
Fire and water.
Seasons
Spring and fall.
Ruling Planets
Neptune and the Sun.
Color
Green.
Gemstone
Coral.
Animals
Seagull, seahorse, and seal.
Ogham Letter
Nion (N).

Symbolism
Power, growth, and leadership.
Correspondences
Aries and Pisces.
Mythology
The Ash tree is one of the highly revered trees among the Celts and is considered the forest's queen. They used its wood to protect them from the fairies and its seeds to perform divination. In some places in Scotland, people used parts of the tree for protection against dark magic. Some Druids used its wood to make their wands. In Norse mythology, the Yggdrasil, the world tree and the center of the universe, was an Ash tree.
Deity
Odin, the Norse god of war and death.
Zodiac
People born under this tree are shy introverts who enjoy spending time alone. This makes them seem mysterious, and many people find them intriguing. When you get to know them, you will find that they are creative individuals with attractive personalities. They don't concern themselves with anything superficial and are often focused on their inner world and vision. They are confident and never bother with other people's opinions about them.

Alder Moon (March 18 – April 14)
Elements
Water and fire.
Season
Spring.
Ruling Planet
Mars.
Color
Red.
Gemstone
Ruby.
Animals

Hawk, fox, and bear.
Ogham Letter
Fearne (F).
Symbolism
Passion, peace, protection, healing, confidence, and determination.
Correspondences
Aries and Pisces.
Mythology
Alder is the tree of wisdom, and it is favored by all the fairies. Bran the Blessed, the mythical king of Britain, used the wood of the Alder to protect him during battle.
Deity
Bran, the god of regeneration.
Zodiac
These people are strong leaders. They are outgoing, charming, and warm individuals who get along with everyone they meet. Others gravitate towards them because they find their confidence infectious. Passionate individuals, they are always working on something, whether to advance in their careers or improve their lives. They prefer to have deep conversations than discuss the weather.

Willow Moon (April 15 – May 12)

Elements
Earth and air.
Seasons
Winter and summer.
Ruling Planet
The Moon.
Color
Yellow.
Gemstone
Moonstone.
Animals
Sea serpent and hare.

Ogham Letter

Saille (S).

Symbolism

Regeneration, fertility, and flexibility.

Correspondences

Taurus and Gemini.

Mythology

The willow tree is associated with growth and healing. The Celts planted it near their homes to protect them against natural disasters.

Deity

Donn, the god of death.

Zodiac

These people are genuine, honest, kind, sympathetic, generous, and decent. They lead quiet lives and steer clear of drama. They are intelligent, loving, peaceful, and have the ability to read others. They are polite individuals who treat everyone with respect. People born under this sign have a great sense of humor and always spread joy wherever they go.

Hawthorn Moon (May 13 – June 9)

Elements

Air and water.

Seasons

Spring and fall.

Ruling Planets

Venus and Mars.

Color

Purple.

Gemstone

Topaz.

Animals

Owl and bee.

Ogham Letter

Huathe (H).

Symbolism
Marriage and purification.

Correspondences
Gemini and cancer.

Mythology
This tree is associated with protection and love. The Celts referred to it as the "Fairy Tree" because these magical creatures guard it. Hence, the people considered it to be sacred and treated it with love and respect.

Deity
Eostre, goddess of spring.

Zodiac
People born under this sign are creative and passionate. Mature individuals, they are prepared to deal with whatever the universe throws at them. Whenever they find someone in trouble, they never hesitate to lend a helping hand. Trustworthy individuals, people often gravitate towards them when they need to vent or share their secrets. They have the ability to see the bigger picture in every situation and deal with all their problems with a big smile.

Oak Moon (June 10 – July 7)

Element
Water.

Season
Summer.

Ruling Planets
Mars and Jupiter.

Color
Black.

Gemstone
Diamond.

Animals
Horse, otter, and wren.

Ogham Letter
Duir (D).
Symbolism
Caring, intuition, strength, and wisdom.
Correspondences
Cancer and Leo,
Mythology
The Celts considered the Oak tree to be the king of the forest. It is associated with myths, rituals, and religion. The Druids revered it highly and held their meetings and rituals under its protection.

In an ancient Celtic legend, there was a king called Math Mathonwy whose dear nephew Lleu Llaw Gyffes was under a terrible curse that prevented him from marrying a human woman, so the king enlisted the help of a sorcerer who went by the name Gwydion to create a beautiful woman for Lleu to marry.

However, she wasn't a real person and never had a normal life which made her weak, and she quickly gave in to temptation. She had an affair with another man, and they both agreed to kill her husband.

Blodeuwedd and her lover attacked Lleu, and he was wounded. He transformed into an eagle and sought refuge in an oak tree until a sorcerer came and cured him. From this day, the oak tree was known as a place for protecting the weak.

Deity
Thor, the Norse god of thunder
Zodiac
These people speak up for those who can't defend themselves. They are patient, calm, generous, and optimistic individuals who believe that things can always get better no matter how bad their circumstances are right now. They are social creatures who are always surrounded by their loved ones.

Holly Moon (July 8 – August 4)

Elements
Water and fire.

Seasons
Summer.

Ruling Planet
Earth.

Color
Silver.

Gemstone
Carnelian.

Animals
Unicorn and cat.

Ogham Letter
Tinne (T).

Symbolism
Optimism, strength, and protection.

Correspondences
Cancer and Leo.

Mythology
The ancient Celts used the wood of the Holly tree in protective spells and to attract good fortune.

Deity
Thor, the god of thunder.

Zodiac
These people are noble individuals who treat others with respect. They are strong and confident, which makes them natural-born leaders. Failure never discourages them. On the contrary, it motivates them to keep going until they achieve their goals. They are warm, kind, and genuine but are often reluctant to let others see this side of them.

Hazel Moon (August 5 – September 1)

Elements

Fire and Earth.

Seasons

Summer.

Ruling Planet

Mercury.

Color

Brown.

Gemstone

Amethyst.

Animals

Salmon and crane.

Ogham Letter

Coll (C).

Symbolism

Divination, knowledge, intuition, and uniqueness.

Correspondences

Leo and Virgo.

Mythology

In Celtic mythology, the fairies lived in the hazel tree, and many people believed its wood to be sacred. They used it for magic and divination. In one legend, the Irish poet Finn Eces was intrigued by the ancient salmon of knowledge. One day, he decided to catch it and feed it to Fionn Mac Cumhaill, the most famous hero in Irish mythology. The fish had acquired his knowledge from eating nuts from the hazel tree and passed it to Fionn.

Zodiac

Quiet individuals, these people prefer to spend time with themselves than in crowds. They are smart and knowledgeable and know how to solve any problem that comes their way. Loyal and sympathetic, their friends can always count on them.

Vine Moon (September 2 – September 29)

Elements
Air and Earth.

Season
Fall.

Ruling Planet
Venus.

Color
Pastel colors.

Gemstone
Emerald.

Animals
Swan, hound, and lizard.

Ogham Letter
Muin (M).

Symbolism
Endurance, opportunity, change, and reward.

Correspondences
Virgo and Libra.

Mythology

In Celtic mythology, the vine tree was a symbol of emotion, initiation, and wisdom. People used its leaves to boost their ambition.

Zodiac

People born under this sign love to be surrounded by beauty. They believe that being better people will benefit them and their community. They have an expensive taste and enjoy spoiling themselves. However, they work hard to support their luxurious lifestyle and share their gifts with the people in their lives. They prefer to stay neutral during disagreements and avoid confrontations.

Ivy Moon (September 30 – October 27)

Elements

Water and air.

Season

Fall.

Ruling Planet

The Moon.

Color

Blue.

Gemstone

Opal.

Animals

Goose, butterfly, and boar.

Ogham Letter

Gort (G).

Symbolism

Love, new opportunities, renewal, and growth.

Correspondences

Libra and Scorpio.

Mythology

The Celts performed rituals to Arianrhod at the ivy tree to open the portal to the underworld, which is also called "the dark side of the moon." Hence, it became a symbol of the mystical and mysterious.

Deity

Arianrhod, goddess of the moon.

Zodiac

These people are witty with unique personalities. Their heads are often in the clouds, and they are generous individuals who love and support the people in their lives. Strong and patient, they never complain even when life gets hard. They rely on their spiritual side to provide them with strength during adversity. Charismatic and charming, they are the life and soul of the party.

Reed Moon (October 28 – November 23)

Elements
Water and fire.
Season
Fall.
Ruling Planet
Pluto.
Color
Orange.
Gemstone
Jasper.
Animals
Owl and hound.
Ogham Letter
Ngetal (N).
Symbolism
Clarity, security, and self-expression.
Correspondences
Scorpio and Sagittarius.
Mythology

The Druids associated the reed tree with learning and wisdom. It can also bring balance to a chaotic world.

Zodiac

They never take things at face value and would dig deep until they find the truth. They are honorable, compassionate, loyal, and confident individuals, and people always love their company. Although they enjoy gossip and can get people to open up to them, these individuals are trustworthy and would never share other people's secrets with anyone.

Elder Moon (November 24 – December 23)

Element
Water.

Season

Winter.

Ruling Planet

Saturn.

Color

Gold.

Gemstone

Jet.

Animals

Raven, horse, badger.

Ogham Letter

Ruis (R).

Symbolism

Magic, death, regeneration, and rebirth.

Correspondences

Sagittarius.

Mythology

In Celtic mythology, the Elder is an enchanted tree that can protect against demons and evil spirits.

Zodiac

People born under this sign have a wild side and enjoy their freedom. They are adventurous and seek new experiences. Supportive and considerate, they help those in need. They are happy individuals who love life, and their positive attitude rubs off on their family and friends. Although they can seem superficial, they are intelligent and deep and often seek answers to life's most complicated questions.

The Celtic tree calendar still fascinates pagans and non-pagans. The use of sacred trees makes it unique and adds a mysterious side to an already interesting system. Its astrology is one of the most exciting parts of this calendar. It will allow you to learn about yourself and the people in your life from a different perspective.

Chapter 5: The Ogham Alphabet

You're probably familiar with the modern-day Roman script of the Irish language. It hasn't always been written like this. The Irish language has gone through various dialects and scripts, many of which you may be familiar with, like the traditional Gaelic format. For the most part, the modern Irish alphabet consists of 26 characters, similar to the English language, and was adapted from the scribal transcriptions of Latin texts, which is why it's somewhat legible and understandable to many people. However, did you know about the existence of another ancient writing system unique to Ireland, particularly associated with the Celts? This script has even less similarities to modern Irish than any other Celtic dialect.

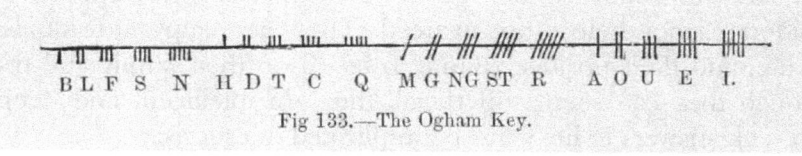

Fig 133.—The Ogham Key.

The Ogham alphabet translated to the English alphabet.
https://commons.wikimedia.org/wiki/File:Ogham_Key_Anderson_1881b_Fig_133_scotlandinearlyc00anderich_0254.jpg

This unique script is known as *Ogham*, which is pronounced as "oh-um." This language is sometimes referred to as the "Celtic Tree Alphabet" and was first discovered in Ireland approximately 1500 years ago. Although this language was initially used to communicate Primitive Irish, it was later modified and adapted for Old Irish and Walsh. Today, only a few manuscripts and inscriptions of this language have been retained, but this doesn't deter scholars from continuing to explore the meanings behind this beautiful language. This script is especially intriguing for those wanting to learn more about Celtic symbolism and also because of its visually expressive nature.

This script is considered to be ancient yet timeless. Why? Because it's still the subject of research for numerous people. The term "Ogham" is said to have been derived from the name "Ogma," which is associated with the Celtic deity known as the God of eloquence. However, the exact origins of the name are still a subject of ongoing debate. This script is also sometimes referred to as Ogam or Ogum. There is a belief held by some scholars that the term "Ogham" actually refers to the individual characters of the script, while the script as a whole is known as "Beith-luis-nin," named after the order of its letters. These letters have visuals unlike any other; each consists of a group of one to five lines arranged vertically over a baseline.

The interesting thing about this script is that it has a controversial history, with its origins still being debated by many people. The obscurity surrounding the history of the Ogham script reflects its ancient origins, as it is shrouded in the mists of time. It is widely regarded as the earliest known written script in Ireland. While some experts attribute its origin to the first century, others believe it was developed in the fourth century. Think of it like this. Ogham is so old that all of its inscriptions are on stone, and it is believed that other inscriptions could have been on sticks, stakes, and trees, which have obviously been lost with time. This chapter will provide an in-depth guide to Ogham, its history, notable features, its relation to Celtic symbolism and divination, and the meanings behind its letters.

Origin Theories

There are contradicting theories when it comes to the origins of Ogham. To be exact, four popular theories attempt to explain the development of the Ogham script. The differences in opinions arise due to the similarities between the Ogham alphabet and other scripts like Germanic runes, elder futhark, Latin, and Greek.

- The first theory proposes that the Irish created Ogham as a cryptic alphabet for political, religious, or military reasons. It was designed to ensure that those who knew only Latin would be unable to understand it.

- The second theory suggests that Ogham was invented by early Christians in Ireland as a means to develop a distinct language. This theory argues that the sounds of Primitive Irish were too difficult to transcribe into Latin, necessitating the creation of a mediating script.
- The third theory claims that Ogham was actually devised in West Wales during the 4th century. Its purpose was to merge and connect the traditional Irish language with the Latin alphabet in response to the intermarriage between the Romans and the Romanized Britons. Bilingual Ogham inscriptions featuring both Irish and Brythonic-Latin alphabets support this theory.
- The fourth theory, initially popular but later overshadowed by other explanations, posits that Ogham was invented around 600 BCE by Gaulish Druids. It was originally an oral and gestural language represented by hand signals. This theory suggests that Ogham was eventually written down in early Christian Ireland, with the lines in the script representing hand gestures or strokes. However, this theory lacks concrete evidence and remains mainly speculative.

Historical Overview

It is believed that Ogham existed as the sole writing system during the Roman Empire, from 400 to 700 AD. Back then, the most commonly used method of communication was through spoken language; even so, Ogham managed to be developed into a written version, albeit a bit late. Particularly, the Celts preferred communicating verbally; according to Julias Caesar, they used to memorize poems instead of writing them down. As a result, Ogham became the first language to be developed from spoken to written word. This script was inscribed into wood, stones, trees, and leaves during this time. Over time, the wooden inscriptions got lost, but there are several impactful stone inscriptions still present in Ireland, acting as a testament to the old language.

As the first ever written language, Ogham wasn't developed further and was only used to depict names and family trees. The stone monuments with Ogham inscriptions are thus believed to be memorials and are suggested to be hero burial grounds. Others believe that these stone monuments were boundary markers or proof of land ownership.

Even though there's only evidence of Ogham in the form of stone inscriptions, many scholars believe that most inscriptions were done on leaves and trees back then. As it happens with every language or technology, the Ogham script was soon phased out when Primitive Irish was replaced by Old Irish. Afterward, the Roman alphabet was adopted and more frequently used, and Ogham's use was no more. However, some suggest that Ogham didn't disappear completely, as there were multiple guides on how to use the Ogham alphabet back in Medieval times.

Ogham inscriptions were primarily carved onto wood or stone, requiring tools like a hammer and chisel to etch messages into the material. As previously mentioned, these inscriptions often served as short memorials to individuals, earning Ogham the classification of a "memorial script." To comprehend these messages, one had to possess knowledge of the twenty characters comprising the Ogham alphabet, along with its intricacies. In the 7th century, five additional characters were introduced to the Ogham alphabet, transforming it into a usable manuscript alphabet. However, this era also marked a turning point for Ogham as it gradually faded from use due to the widespread adoption of Latin.

The investigation into the history and meanings of this enigmatic alphabet began with the discovery of the Mount Callan stone in 1785. This finding sparked the interest of archaeologists and linguists, initiating the quest to unravel the secrets of Ogham inscriptions. At first, Ogham inscriptions were mistaken for Egyptian Hieroglyphics but were later classified as different. Many connections were made with the discoveries of different stone monuments with Ogham inscriptions. The Celts were also attached to Ogham by some spectators.

Features of Ogham

Ogham is a beautiful, albeit complicated script with 25 letters grouped into five sections of five letters each. Each of these sections was named after the first letter, and the five sections total about 80 Gaelic sounds, although it's not yet decided why these sounds were grouped together in their respective sequences. It is worth mentioning that the second group is composed of stop consonants, with the exception of /h/, whereas the fourth group exclusively consists of vowels. Each letter's affiliation to a specific group can be easily determined due to its shared visual features.

The initial set of letters consists of right-sided marks, whereas the subsequent set displays left-sided marks. The third group has diagonal lines, while the fourth section features lines intersecting the central line, flowing from left to right. Interestingly, the vowels within the fourth group can alternatively be represented by dots rather than lines. Finally, the fifth group stands as the most intricate of all, with distinct symbols instead of mere linear markings. This complexity arises from the inclusion of letters introduced after 600 AD, reflecting advancements in the Irish language. Occasionally, arrowheads were utilized to indicate sentence beginnings and endings.

The Ogham Alphabet

1. B - Beith

Beith, the first letter of the Ogham alphabet.
https://commons.wikimedia.org/wiki/File:Ogham_letter_beith.svg

Beth or Beith represents the letter B in the alphabet and is linked to the birch tree. The significance of this letter is connected to fresh starts, liberation, transitions, metamorphosis, and renewal. When this symbol emerges, it serves as a reminder to let go of negativity and prioritize the positive aspects of your life.

2. L – Luis

Luis, the second letter in the Ogham alphabet.
https://commons.wikimedia.org/wiki/File:Ogham_letter_luis.svg

Luis corresponds to the letter L in the alphabet and is associated with the Rowan tree. This letter symbolizes blessings, safeguarding, and gaining wisdom. The Rowan tree is renowned for its mystical protection against enchantments or magical influences. The essence of this letter encourages embracing your spiritual beliefs and maintaining a strong foundation, especially during times of uncertainty. Have faith in your own discernment and avoid being deceived by false security.

3. F – Fearn

Fearn, the third letter of the Ogham alphabet.
https://commons.wikimedia.org/wiki/File:Ogham_letter_fearn.svg

Fearn or Fern is the equivalent of the letter F and is linked to the Alder tree. This dynamic tree represents a spirit that is continuously growing and is associated with the spring equinox. In Celtic folklore, Alder is symbolized by the courageous Bran, who acted as a bridge over a river to ensure the safety of others. Similarly, the Alder tree bridges the mystical realm between heaven and earth. When you come across this symbol, strive to be a mediator between individuals in conflict. Trust your intuition, and others will naturally seek your guidance.

4. S – Saille

Saille is associated with the Willow tree.
https://commons.wikimedia.org/wiki/File:Ogham_letter_sail.svg

S or Saille is associated with the Willow tree, which is usually found near water. This letter symbolizes the knowledge and spiritual growth of a person and offers protection and healing. Saille's correspondences are that you cannot evolve without changing first and realizing that change is a part of life. So, give yourself a break, and take some time to rest spiritually.

5. N – Nion

Nion is linked to the Ash tree.
https://commons.wikimedia.org/wiki/File:Ogham_letter_nion.svg

The letter N corresponds to Nion, which is linked to the Ash tree. Within Celtic heritage, the Ash tree holds sacred significance for the Druids, as it represents a connection between the inner and outer realms. This letter serves as a symbol of interconnectivity, creative energy, and transitions. When you encounter this symbol, it serves as a reminder that every action, no matter how small, carries consequences. Your choices and deeds have an impact on the future, extending beyond the present moment.

6. H – Huath

Huath symbolizes the Hawthorn trees.
https://commons.wikimedia.org/wiki/File:Ogham_letter_uath.svg

H symbolizes Huath, the Hawthorn tree, representing cleansing, protection, and defense. In corporal aspects, it signifies fertility, offering protection, health, and self-defense. In magical aspects, it teaches that spiritual strength can navigate thorny challenges and provide support to others.

7. D – Duir

Duir symbolizes the Celtic Oak tree.
https://commons.wikimedia.org/wiki/File:Ogham_letter_dair.svg

The letter D corresponds to Duir, which is associated with the Celtic Oak tree, symbolizing qualities of strength, resilience, and self-confidence. Carrying an acorn is said to bring luck in interviews and business meetings. Similar to this, it is believed that capturing a falling oak leaf will bring health in the upcoming year. The word "Duir" itself, which means "gate" or "door," conveys the significance of taking advantage of unanticipated chances and possibilities. From a magical perspective, embodying the unwavering steadfastness of the Oak empowers one to overcome spiritual challenges with unwavering strength.

8. T – Tinne

Tinne represents the Holly tree.
https://commons.wikimedia.org/wiki/File:Ogham_letter_tinne.svg

The letter T corresponds to Tinne, which represents the Holly tree in Celtic symbolism. Immortality, harmony, bravery, and the stability of the home are all associated with the holly tree. Together, we may find strength and safety through the values of trust and honor. It is crucial to develop quick and shrewd perception when it comes to magical significance. The key to reacting to novel spiritual circumstances is flexibility and agility. Trust your instincts when it comes to maintaining a balanced strategy that balances the emotions and the mind.

9. C – Coll

Coll is associated with wisdom and creativity.
https://commons.wikimedia.org/wiki/File:Ogham_letter_coll.svg

The letter C, or K, stands for Coll, the Hazel tree related to knowledge, creativity, and wisdom. In August, known as the Hazel Moon, the tree bears nuts symbolizing the life force within. In Celtic mythology, hazel is associated with enchanted springs, holy wells, and divination. Whatever your creative talents are, look for inspiration. In magical aspects, allow the divine to guide your creative journey, invoking the gods for inspiration and calling upon a Muse when needing a creative spark.

10. Q – Quert

Quert represents the Apple tree.
https://commons.wikimedia.org/wiki/File:Ogham_letter_ceirt.svg

Q represents Quert, or Ceirt, which stands for the apple tree. The apple is a traditional representation of love, loyalty, and rebirth that is frequently linked to magic. In mundane aspects, making choices can be challenging. Sometimes the right decision may not bring immediate happiness, but wisdom lies in discerning what is truly needed. In magical aspects, embrace new decisions and reap the spiritual gifts they offer. Trust that valuable lessons will be learned along the way – even when things seem unclear.

11. M – Muin

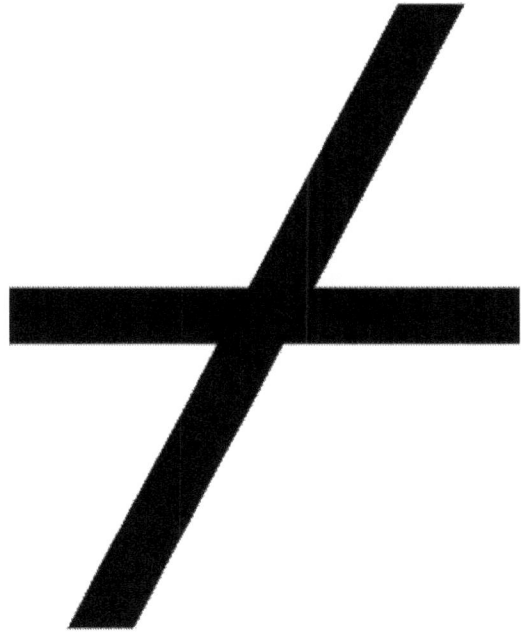

Muin represents the Vine.
https://commons.wikimedia.org/wiki/File:Ogham_letter_muin.svg

The letter M corresponds to Muin, representing the Vine in Celtic symbolism. The Vine is associated with inward journeys and life lessons, serving as the source of grapes and wine. In terms of magical significance, it encourages engagement in prophecy and divination rituals. It is advisable to keep a record of received messages, as their meaning may become clear at a later time. When enjoying the pleasures associated with the Vine, it is important to remain mindful and avoid overindulgence, as excessive indulgence can distort one's perception of truth.

12. G – Gort

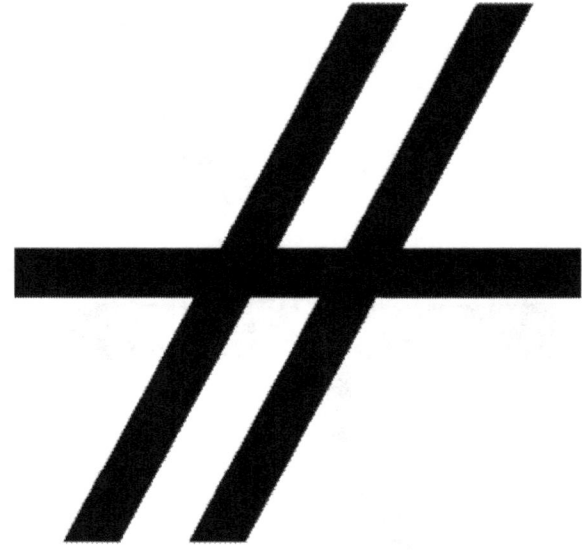

Gort represents the Ivy.
https://commons.wikimedia.org/wiki/File:Ogham_letter_gort.svg

The letter G corresponds to Gort, representing the Ivy in Celtic symbolism. Ivy is known for its ability to grow independently and parasitically on other plants. It thrives in diverse conditions and symbolizes the soul's journey of self-discovery across different realms. Gort is associated with growth, untamed energy, and exploring mystical aspects of personal development. Additionally, it is connected to October and the Samhain sabbat. In the physical realm, encountering Gort signifies the importance of eliminating negativity and toxic relationships from your life. In terms of magical significance, it urges you to seek internal personal growth and seek spiritual companionship externally. If you come across Gort, it might be worth considering joining or forming a group of like-minded individuals to embark on this journey together.

13. Ng – nGeatal

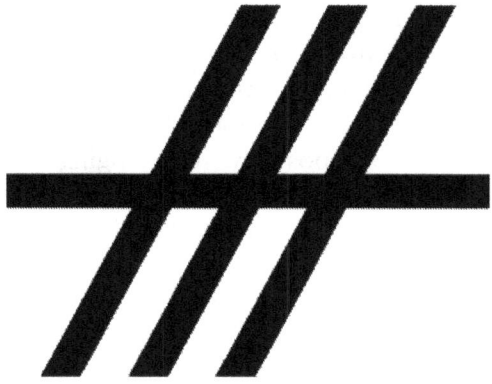

nGeatal represents the Reeds that grow by riversides.
https://commons.wikimedia.org/wiki/File:Ogham_letter_ngeadal.svg

Ng, or nGeatal, represents the Reed that grows tall by riversides. It symbolizes direct action and purpose in one's journey. Associated with music, health, and joyful gatherings, the Reed signifies taking leadership roles, rebuilding, and making proactive decisions. In magical aspects, it highlights fruitful spiritual growth through challenges and the importance of learning valuable lessons along the path.

14. St – Straith

Straith corresponds to the Blackthorn tree.
https://commons.wikimedia.org/wiki/File:Ogham_letter_straif.svg

In Celtic iconography, the letter *St,* also spelled Straith or Straif, stands for the Blackthorn tree. Blackthorn is a symbol of power, mastery, and triumph over adversity. In everyday life, encountering Straith signifies the need to anticipate the unexpected and be prepared for changes that may disrupt your plans. It serves as a reminder that external forces can significantly impact your path. From a magical perspective, coming across this symbol indicates the beginning of a new journey where surprises, possibly challenging ones, lie ahead. Overcoming these obstacles will grant you strength and resilience. Embrace the understanding that both you and your life are undergoing transformation during this time.

15. R – Ruis

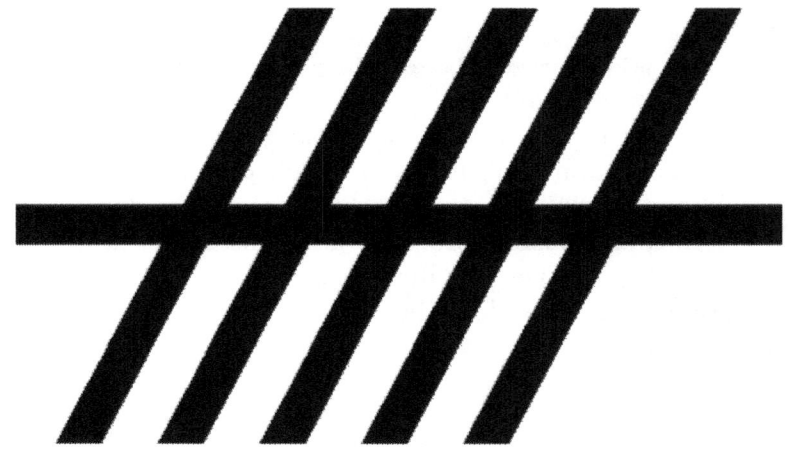

Ruis is associated with the Winter Solstice.
https://commons.wikimedia.org/wiki/File:Ogham_letter_ruis.svg

R is the Elder tree known as Ruis, which is connected to the Winter Solstice. Elder signifies endings, maturity, and wisdom gained through experience. In daily aspects, embrace the transition between phases of life, recognizing the value of maturity and knowledge. Strive for childlike wonder while avoiding childish behavior. Magically, expect new growth stages and experiences that result in spiritual regeneration and eventual rebirth. Understand that every experience contributes to shaping the person you are destined to become.

16. A – Ailim

Ailim represents the Elm tree.
https://commons.wikimedia.org/wiki/File:Ogham_letter_ailm.svg

    The Celtic emblem for the Elm tree, Ailim, often spelled Ailm, is represented by the letter A. The Fir or Pine tree is also included in this symbol. These mighty forest giants are significant because they provide us perspective and enable us to stand above our surroundings. It signals the need to consider the bigger picture and long-term goals in real life. Be prepared for what lies ahead and embrace a broader perspective. In magical aspects, mark your spiritual growth and progress. Look to the future and envision where your newfound wisdom will lead you. Be open to guiding others who follow your path and extend a helping hand when needed.

17. - Onn

Onn symbolizes the Gorse bush.
https://commons.wikimedia.org/wiki/File:Ogham_letter_onn.svg

The Gorse bush, also known as Furze, is symbolized by the letter O, alternatively spelled Onn or Ohn. In life, it represents what you've been seeking is within reach, so persist in pursuing your goals. If you're unsure of your path, create a list of goals to clarify your direction and focus on the journey. In magical aspects, your spiritual journey has bestowed abundant gifts on you. Share these blessings with others and embrace leadership or mentoring opportunities that come your way.

18. U – Uhr

Ur represents the Heather plant.
https://commons.wikimedia.org/wiki/File:Ogham_letter_ur.svg

The Celtic emblem for the Heather plant, Uhr or Ura, is represented by the letter U. Heather represents zeal and charity. In the Celtic moors, this tough shrub lives on peat. In life, this symbol calls for destressing and seeking inner healing for the body. Listen to your physical needs and recognize the interconnectedness of physical well-being and emotional health. In magical aspects, integrate spiritual energy with physical healing. To cultivate a healthy soul, emphasize holistic healing of the body, mind, and spirit.

19. E - Eadhadh

Eadhadh symbolizes the Aspen tree.
https://commons.wikimedia.org/wiki/File:Ogham_letter_eadhadh.svg

He represents the Aspen tree, which stands for fortitude and bravery, and is called Eadhadh or Eadha. When you encounter this symbol, emulate the resilience of the Aspen, staying flexible in the face of obstacles. Trust that challenges are transient, leaving you stronger. Overcome fears and reservations for personal growth. In magical aspects, resist succumbing to worldly pressures. Shift your focus to your spiritual journey, even when it feels tempting to give up.

20. I - Iodhadh

Iodhadh represents the Yew tree.
https://commons.wikimedia.org/wiki/File:Ogham_letter_iodhadh.svg

The Celtic emblem for the Yew tree, Iodhadh or Idad, relates to the letter I. Because it resembles the Tarot's Death card, the Yew tree is frequently linked to concepts of death and endings. In the physical world, the appearance of Iodhadh indicates significant transitions. Embrace awareness of these changes, understanding that while not all may be negative, they will likely be substantial. Clear out unnecessary things to make room for fresh beginnings. In magical aspects, release attachment to beliefs and ideas that no longer serve you. Embrace the transformative power of change, seeing it as an opportunity rather than an obstacle. Welcome new experiences without fear and embrace the unknown.

The Ogham alphabet stands as a testament to the rich tapestry of Celtic symbolism. Its distinctive arrangement of notches and lines perfectly captures the profound connection between language, nature, and spirituality that was deeply ingrained in the Celtic culture. The Ogham script, with its roots in the ancient Celtic lands, serves as a bridge between the material and the mystical, offering a glimpse into the beliefs and wisdom of the Celts. The Ogham alphabet's association with trees and the natural world underscores the Celts' reverence for their environment. Each character corresponds to a specific tree, reflecting the interdependence between humanity and the natural realm. This intimate relationship with nature finds expression through the Ogham script, making it a unique writing system that encapsulates the Celtic worldview.

Chapter 6: The Wheel of the Year

Now that you understand the Celtic tree calendar and how it works, this chapter will focus on the ancient Irish festivals that are still popular among many Neo-pagans. These festivities celebrate nature, mark the changing of the seasons, and honor your connection with the natural world. There are eight in the Celtic wheel of the year that begins with the festival of Samhain and ends with the festival of Mabon.

The wheel of the year goes by many names: the eight Sabbats, the witches' wheel, the pagan wheel, the Irish wheel, the sacred wheel, and the Celtic wheel. It represents the seasonal cycle and festivals that the Celts celebrated at the beginning of each season. Unlike the Celtic tree system, the wheel is a solar calendar representing the cycle of plants beginning with sprouting seeds, then plants budding, blooming, and fruiting, and finally turning to seeds and repeating the cycle. Similar to the wheel, it is always turning.

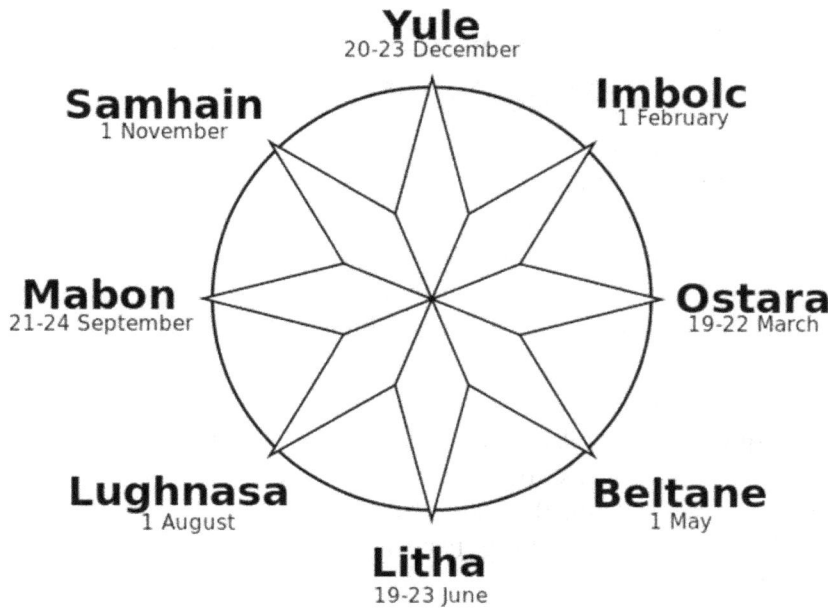

The wheel of the year.
User: The Wednesday Island, after en:User: Brenton.eccles, Public domain, via Wikimedia Commons: https://commons.wikimedia.org/wiki/File:Wheel_of_the_Year.svg

The main purpose of the wheel of the year is to connect you with nature, the cycle of the seasons, and the spirits of your ancestors, like with the festival of Samhain. It is about celebrating Mother Earth rather than honoring a specific god or goddess.

Similar to the tree calendar, the wheel of the year also represents the ongoing cycle of life: birth, death, and rebirth. However, this doesn't only apply to mankind but to nature as well. It withers and dies in the fall and winter to be reborn again in the spring and summer.

Some people think the wheel of the year is Wiccan since it celebrates and honors some pagan deities, but this isn't true. However, pagans and non-pagans can celebrate these festivals whether they worship Celtic or Wiccan deities or not.

This chapter will discuss the wheel of the year and the eight Celtic festivals, and all practices and traditions associated with them,

The Solstice and Equinox Festivals on the Wheel of the Year

The fall and spring equinoxes and the summer and winter solstice are called "The Quarter Points" and are located on the east, west, north, and south points of the wheel of the year. These points are also called "solar days" since they mark the time when the sun is at its strongest in the sky and the longest day of the year. Similarly, they can also mark the days when the sun is at its weakest in the skies and the shortest day of the year. The solstice festivals are Yule/Midwinter (December 21st) and Litha/Midsummer (June 21st).

The equinox takes place when the sun passes the equator, and the days become as long as the nights. The word "equinox" is of Latin origin. It is derived from the words "*aequus*" and "*nox*" meaning equal and night, respectively. These festivals are Ostara (March 21st) and Mabon (Sept 21st).

The cross-quarter points refer to the festivals that take place between the solstice and the equinoxes during the peak of the four seasons.

These festivals are often called the four great fire festivals or major sabbats, and they are:

- Samhain
- Imbolc
- Beltane
- Lughnasadh

Similar to zodiac signs, the quarter points on the wheel of the year are associated with the four elements.

- North is Earth
- South is fire
- East is air
- West is water

There is a fifth element at the center of the wheel called source or spirit, and it represents the invisible world that exists around you, like the soul that brings you to life and the love that unites the whole world together.

These five elements are significant in Celtic mythology and spiritual traditions. They are associated with sacred places, spirits of nature, and deities. For this reason, the ancient Celts highly revered them. Each of the eight festivals is also associated with types of crystals, colors, herbs, and plants.

The History of the Celtic Festivals

In France, historians discovered a Celtic calendar that showed the ancient Irish celebrating four fire festivals that honor the sun's movements throughout the seasons. These festivals include two equinoxes and two solstices. When the ancient Saxons and Germanic peoples intertwined with the Celts, they introduced them to the other four festivals. The eight festivals make the wheel of the year, and each one of them is celebrated every month and a half.

Although the ancient Celts and Neo-pagans celebrate these festivals to honor nature, the wheel of the year was specifically significant to the ancient Celtic farmers. They depended on it to mark seasonal changes to determine when to plow, sow, and harvest their produce.

The names of the Celtic festivals are derived from ancient cultures like the Germanic, Anglo-Saxon, Norse, and Celtic.

The Spiritual Significance of the Wheel of the Year

The wheel of the year alternates between festivals that celebrate the changes of the seasons or festivals that are inspired by ancient traditions. The Celts celebrated these occasions by providing offerings to their deities and thanking them for all their gifts. These seasonal cycles taught them that change was necessary, a significant part of nature and life to be accepted and embraced. They used this time to connect with their spiritual side and perform specific rituals to honor nature.

These festivals represent the unity between the natural and the supernatural, the spiritual and the physical world.

For many people, the solstice is a time for self-reflection since it takes place after the first half of the year. You can think about what you have achieved in the last six months and where you hope to end up by the end of the year. On the other hand, the equinox is about bringing balance to your life as you observe the equal length of the day and night and darkness and light.

The four great fire festivals allow you to enjoy life and be grateful for all the blessings nature bestows upon you each season. It is a time to connect with Mother Earth during the highest point of her seasonal cycles.

Now that you have learned about the year's wheel, the chapter's second part will focus on each of the eight seasonal festivals.

Samhain (October 31st)

Pronunciation

In Ireland, Samhain is pronounced as "Sow-wen."

Colors

Orange, gold, silver, purple, and black.

Crystals

Onyx, Bloodstone, Smokey Quartz, and Clear Quartz.

Plants and Herbs

Sage, nutmeg, garlic, rosemary, and Calendula.

Food and Drinks

Pumpkin, meat, potatoes, apples, and parsnips.

Incense

Myrrh, cinnamon, mint, frankincense, and sage.

Meaning

In Gaelic, the word "Samhain" means "end of summer." This day marks the New Year in Celtic traditions and the beginning of the wheel of the year. The Celts believed that during this time, the veil between the world of the living and the realm of the dead was at its weakest, and the spirits could roam freely between the two worlds. Although this can sound like the plot of a scary movie, for the Celts, this thought provided them with comfort. They were happy knowing the spirits of their ancestors and their departed loved ones would come and visit.

However, some of these spirits might have returned for vengeance against a person who wronged them or was responsible for their death. In this case, some people wore masks to hide from them.

It wasn't only the spirits of the dead who visited the realm of the living, but all creatures from the otherworld, such as fairies, crossed over. People protected themselves from these entities by wearing customs to hide their identities.

Practice and Rituals

Samhain rituals include feasting, dancing, building altars for the ancestors and presenting offerings, wearing masks, and carving pumpkins. Ancient Celts also had silent suppers by placing an extra seat and dish at the dining table for their dead ancestor or a departed loved one and eating in silence. They welcomed the spirits by cooking their favorite meals, leaving treats outside, and putting candles in their window to guide them.

You are correct if you feel that Samhain's rituals are quite similar to Halloween. The modern holiday is based on the ancient Celtic celebration.

Yule/Winter Solstice (December 20-23)

Pronunciation

Yule is pronounced as "Yool."

Colors

Gold, green, and red

Crystals

Clear quartz, citrine, emerald, and bloodstone.

Plants and Herbs

Oak leaves, nutmeg, cloves, cinnamon, fir, and pine.

Food and Drinks

Nuts, hot cider, wine, and soup.

Incense

Pine, cinnamon, Frankincense, and cedar.

Meaning

The festival of Yule represents rebirth, renewal, and growth. It falls on the coldest and shortest day of the year, which is referred to as the *winter solstice*. Since the Celts and Druids highly revered trees, they celebrated Yule by going outside and decorating evergreen trees, which they believed were symbols of life and survival.

Yule is also a celebration of the Oak King's victory over his brother, the Holy King. The two brothers symbolize the four seasons. King Holy ruled over Earth for the first part of the year when it was cold and dark.

However, as the days became longer, King Oak came back to life, killed his brother, and reigned over Earth.

Practice and Rituals

Many people practice Yule rituals by burning a Yule log, decorating a tree, hanging a mistletoe, making a wreath, lighting candles, preparing a feast, exchanging gifts, and building an altar. People also burned bonfires representing the sun's return since days became longer after Yule. They also celebrate this festival by singing and burning a fire where families and friends gather to throw holly to symbolize leaving the past behind and embracing the future.

The logs used in these rituals should be cut, not bought. You should also save a piece of it to burn in the next Yule as a symbol of continuity.

Christmas rituals and traditions were also borrowed from Yule.

Imbolc (February 2nd)

Pronunciation

Imbolc is pronounced as "ˈɪmbʊlk."

Colors

Light green, white, and pink.

Crystals

Bloodstone, citrine, turquoise, Amethyst.

Plants and Herbs

Witch hazel, snowdrops, cinnamon, chamomile, and blackberry.

Food and Drinks

Oats, bread, pumpkin seeds, and sunflowers.

Incense

Chamomile, jasmine, lily, and vanilla.

Meaning

Imbolc is derived from the old Irish word "*oimelc*," meaning "inside the belly" or "sheep's milk," and it represents pregnant sheep. It signifies Mother Earth's womb, where spring emerges from. This is the time of year when flowers, trees, and all other plants awaken from their long slumber.

This festival takes place between the winter solstice and the spring equinox. It represents fertility, rebirth, hope, purification, and better days.

Imbolc celebrates Brigid, the goddess of fertility, spring, poetry, and medicine. It marks the end of the cold and dark winter and welcomes spring and the agricultural season. Imbolc is a time for new beginnings and growth.

Practice and Rituals

People celebrate by lighting bonfires for purification and to honor the sun. They also make Brigid dolls or crosses from corn stalks and hang them on their doors or inside their homes. People also placed a broom at their front door to symbolize sweeping out the past and all the things that no longer serve them to make space for the future and all it has to offer.

Ostara/Spring Equinox (March 20-23)

Pronunciation

Osatra is pronounced as "oh s t aa er."

Colors

Shades of green, pink, yellow, and white.

Crystals

Rose quartz, amethyst, and aquamarine.

Plans and herbs

Snowdrops, tulips, crocus, daffodils, catnip, spearmint, lemongrass, clover, and meadowsweet.

Food and Drinks

Honey, bread, lettuce, spinach, kale, and eggs.

Incense

Narcissus, violet, jasmine, sandalwood, strawberry, and rose.

Meaning

Ostara is derived from "Eostre," the goddess of dawn and spring, and it celebrates the arrival of spring and new beginnings. In Celtic mythology, Eostre awoke from her long slumber on Ostara and resurfaced from under the ground. In another myth, the festival honors the day the goddess became pregnant with the god of the sun, who was born on Yule. Some traditions combine the two myths together.

Ostara is associated with rebirth, new life, fertility, and balance since day and night, light and dark, are equal. This is a time that gives people hope as they witness the arrival of spring after the dark and cold winter.

Practice and Rituals

People celebrate this festival by throwing feasts, lighting fires, coloring, and decorating eggs. This festival is associated with Easter, which is why they both have similar rituals and practices.

Beltane (May 1st)

Pronunciation

Beltane is pronounced as "beltayn."

Colors

Yellow, green, blue, and red.

Crystals

Rose quartz, malachite, beryl, sunstone, emerald.

Plants and Herbs

Rose, oak, primrose, paprika, meadowsweet, dandelion, hawthorne, and daffodil.

Food and Drinks

Cakes, oats, elderflower, sweet bread, and wine.

Incense

Vanilla, peach, ylang-ylang, frankincense, and rose.

Meaning

This festival marks the beginning of summer, celebrating fertility and light. The word Beltane means "Bel's fire," Bel means bright fire, and it is also the name of the Celtic god of the sun. This is the time when the day becomes longer than the night and all-natural and supernatural beings like spirits and fairies awaken from their slumber. With its burning hot fire, Beltane is associated with passion and lust.

Practices and Rituals

People celebrate Beltane by building a fairy altar, making a flower crown, praying, maypole dancing, and holding weddings. They also burn bonfires, symbolizing passion, letting go of your inhibitions, and following your heart's desire. The ancient Celts also celebrated Beltane by dancing in nature around trees. They would also dress a young girl in colorful clothes and place a wreath of flowers over her head to symbolize the goddess of spring.

The ancient Celts placed a brown branch in their homes to protect them against the fairies or other supernatural entities that awoke. Many people also get married on this day since it is associated with passion.

Litha/Summer Solstice (June 20th-23rd)
Pronunciation
Litha is pronounced just like it's written, and the "th" are soft.
Colors
Orange, yellow, gold, and red.
Crystals
Emerald, yellow topaz, calcite, citrine, and sunstone.
Plants and Herbs
Verbena, thyme, rosemary, mint, chamomile, calendula, mugwort, mullein, lavender, sage, rose, sunflower, and dandelions.
Food and Drinks
Honey, carrots, squash, ice cream, and apple cider.
Incense
Sage, lemon, orange, musk, lavender, and rose.
Meaning
Litha marks the longest day of the year when the sun is at its peak. It is also when the sun's heat begins to weaken, and the day becomes shorter. This festival takes place in the middle of the summer when nature is at its strongest, the days are warm, and the plants are flourishing.

In Celtic mythology, the Oak King gave up his kingdom to his brother, the Holy King, during Litha. It is a special occasion that honors the victory of light over darkness. It is also a symbol that no matter how dark or hard life gets, things will always get better, and the sun will shine again.

The word "*Litha*" is of Anglo-Saxon origin and means June.
Practices and Rituals
This festival is celebrated by burning bonfires, feasting, eating fresh fruits, and dancing. Ancient Celts practiced certain rituals to protect

themselves against the supernatural creatures who re-emerged during Beltane since they became very powerful on Litha and could spread chaos and cause harm.

Lughnasadh (August 1st)

Pronunciation

Lughnasadh is pronounced as "LOO-nuss-uh."

Colors

Yellow, light brown, gold, and green.

Crystals

Peridot, tiger's eye, amber, golden topaz, citrine.

Plants and Herbs

Ivy, clover, blackthorn, basil, Heather, and grains.

Incense

Frankincense, rose, mint, and sandalwood.

Meaning

Lughnasadh celebrates the harvest season and marks the period between summer and fall. It is named after Lugh, the god of light and the sun, because of a legend that links him to this festival.

Lugh's mother, Tailtiu, the goddess of Sovereignty, cared more about mankind and their wellbeing than herself. She spent her days preparing the lands for cultivation. However, she worked so hard that her body couldn't take it anymore and died. Every year, Lugh would honor his mother with a lavish feast which came to be known as Lughnasadh.

This festival takes place in the last few months of the year, so it's an opportunity to reap the benefits of all your hard work. It is time for self-reflection and asking yourself if you have achieved all your goals or if you should assess your choices and decisions and make adjustments.

Practices and Rituals

The ancient Celts would present offerings from their harvest to their gods and goddesses on Lughnasadh. They would also honor Tailtiu by playing sports like boxing and wrestling. People also celebrated by lighting bonfires and getting married.

Mabon/Autumn Equinox (September 20th-23rd)

Pronunciation

Mabon is pronounced as "maybn."

Colors

Orange, yellow, gold, and brown.

Crystals

Lapis lazuli, sapphire, quartz, amber, and citrine.

Plants and Herbs

Marigold, chamomile, rosemary, and sage.

Incense

Frankincense, apple, cinnamon, pine, and sage.

Meaning

Mabon is the last festival on the wheel of the year. It is a time to reflect on your losses and gains. Although celebrating the autumn equinox is an ancient tradition, the name *Mabon* is relatively new. Wiccan writer Aidan Kelly came up with it. He named the festival after Mabon and Modron, the Welsh hunter god.

The festival marks the loss of the Celtic fertility god Cernnunos who went to the underworld every year during the autumn equinox and re-emerged as the green man to symbolize rebirth and growth,

Practices and Rituals

People celebrated Mabon by setting up an altar to honor Cernunnos and expressing their gratitude for their harvest and all the blessings nature bestowed upon them.

Each festival on the wheel of the year has its own unique name and rituals. However, there is one thing they all share in common – nature. Most people take nature and the changing of the seasons for granted, but can you imagine what the world would be like if there was only one season?

Change is necessary, and each season is a reminder that nothing in life lasts. It is a comforting thought knowing that light will always come after darkness. However, it also reminds you that sunny and warm days won't last forever, so cherish them and enjoy them for as long as they last.

Remember, the wheel of the year will always keep turning, and good days will come sooner or later.

Chapter 7: The Tree of Life

Have you ever seen an Irish person wearing a tree pendant? You probably thought it was a random piece of jewelry, but what you may not know is that this is no ordinary tree. It is The Tree of Life, one of the most significant symbols in Celtic mythology. It represents the essence of life, a popular concept that has appeared in many mythologies, religions, and cultures throughout history. The concept of the tree of life exists in different beliefs and faiths.

The Celtic tree of life.
Art Gongs, CC BY-SA 4.0 <https://creativecommons.org/licenses/by-sa/4.0>, via Wikimedia Commons: https://commons.wikimedia.org/wiki/File:Celtic_Tree_Of_Life_Art_Gong.jpg

Although many ancient cultures used this symbol, it held a special meaning among the Celts, who, in turn, influenced their Irish descendants. Even though it's hundreds of years old, people still cherish it and use it in jewelry, painting, decorations, etc.

The Celts and the Druids highly revered trees. They appeared in different parts of their mythology, like the Celtic tree calendar. Trees also played a huge role in their daily lives. They were a source of food, medicine, and shelter, and they burned their wood to keep them warm during the winter. It is no wonder that the Druids considered them to be sacred. Trees have always been a source of life, and the ancient Irish depended on them in all aspects of their lives.

In Celtic mythology, trees had a spiritual significance; they acted as portals between the world of the living and the spiritual realm. The Druids also believed that the spirits of their ancestors lingered in trees which made them enchanted. Hence, they turned to their sacred trees during tough times or whenever they needed assistance. The Druids also presented offerings to the gods and chose their chiefs under trees.

The ancient Celts associated the tree of life with the forces of nature as they come together to create balance and harmony for mankind and the universe. It also represented strength, knowledge, power, wisdom, and protection. It encompassed all the natural and spiritual elements necessary for life on Earth.

The Tree of Life is a complex and multi-layered symbol that reflects ancient Irish culture and traditions. It represents stability, strength, and faith, and the Druids and Celts believed it to be the center of the universe.

This chapter will detail the significance of the Tree of Life, its different parts, and what each one symbolizes.

The History of the Tree of Life

It isn't an exaggeration to say that this symbol is as old as human beings. In Norse Mythology, the Vikings brought their Tree of Life with them when they came to Ireland, which could have influenced the Celts to create their own. It is believed that the ancient Egyptians were the first people to create and use this symbol. It was found carved on their tombs and other monuments as well. In other words, the Celts weren't the ones who invented the concept of the Tree of Life since it existed centuries before the ancient Irish civilization came to be.

While all countries and faiths consider the Tree of Life to be sacred, each assigned a different meaning to it based on their own beliefs and ideologies.

The Tree of Life in Greek and Roman Mythology

In Greek and Roman mythology, the Tree of Life is quite similar to the Celtic tree as its roots reach out to the underworld, and its branches reach to the stars or the heavens.

The Tree of Life in Ancient Egypt

The ancient Egyptians believed that the branches of the Tree of Life represented abundance and the heavens, while its roots symbolized death. In ancient Egyptian Mythology, Isis, the goddess of magic and wisdom, and Osiris, the god of death and rebirth, sprung from the Tree of Life.

The Tree of Life in Norse Mythology

The Tree of Life is also called Yggdrasil or the Viking Tree of Life. It is an ash tree and one of the most sacred symbols in Norse mythology. The Nine Worlds of the universe stood on its branches. If anything happened to this tree, the world would perish.

The Tree of Life in China

There is a famous story in Chinese mythology about an enchanted peach tree that grows fruits once every three thousand years. Whoever eats one of its fruits will be immortal. This Chinese Tree of Life is depicted differently from its Celtic counterpart. It has a phoenix at the top and a dragon at the bottom.

The Tree of Life in Mayan Civilization

The Mayans believed that when the universe was created, there was a large tree that connected the otherworld, the physical world, and heaven together. Everything in life came from this tree. This is the Tree of Life and the origin of the universe.

The Tree of Life in Buddhism

The Buddhists believe Buddha attained enlightenment while sitting under the Tree of Life, Bodhi. In Buddhism, this sacred tree represents existence and enlightenment.

Hinduism

Hindus believe their Tree of Life grows upside down; its branches are underground while its roots reach the sky. This tree blesses people and provides them with what they need to survive.

The Tree of Life in African Culture

In Africa, the Tree of Life is the Baobab tree. Although the climate in this area is dry and some plants struggle to grow, there is always fruit growing on this sacred tree. For this reason, the African people highly revere it since it is the source of nourishment and life.

The Tree of Life In Bahrain

Interestingly, in Bahrain, there is a tree in the middle of the desert standing tall in the hot and dry weather. It is over four hundred years old, and no one knows how it survived all these years since there isn't any water source close to it. It is a miraculous tree that represents power and magic. The locals refer to it as the Tree of Life.

The Tree of Life in Christianity

The Bible mentions the story of Adam and Eve and how they disobeyed God and ate from the forbidden tree. It is believed to be the Tree of Life, symbolizing God's love and wisdom.

The Tree of Life in Islam

The Forbidden Tree or Tree of Immortality is also mentioned in the Quran. Other trees in Islam resemble the Tree of Life: The Tree of Knowledge, The Infernal Tree, and The Lote Tree.

The Tree of Life in Kabbalah

In Kabbalah, a mystic branch of Judaism, the Tree of Life is a symbol or illustration, not a real tree. It connects mankind with the angel and the Divine.

The Tree of Life in Native America

Similar to the Celts, the Native Americans have many myths and legends about their sacred trees and assign a meaning to each one of them. In one of these stories, they talked about a giant tree that connected the spirit realm, the physical world, and the heavens together. This is the Tree of Life.

The Tree of Life in Celtic Mythology

The Celts and the Druids believed that trees connected them to their families, dead ancestors, and their gods and goddesses. They believed that the Tree of Life was a symbol of the afterlife and connected them to the world of the spirits and the heavens.

Myth about the Tree of Life

The Tree of Life is featured in many Irish myths and legends, but there is one tale that reflects the significance of the tree; it is the myth of the founding of Ireland.

There was a giant called Treochair who lived in the Otherworld. He brought a branch from the Tree of Life to Earth one day. He shook it a couple of times, and acorns, apples, and nuts fell from it. He then planted them in the north, south, east, west, and center of the Emerald Isle. Hence, the five sacred trees that protect and guard Ireland were created from the Tree of Life.

It's an Oak Tree

The Celts often described the Tree of Life as an oak tree since it is one of the world's most ancient, majestic, and powerful trees. If you observe any oak tree, you will notice that it is huge and one of the tallest trees you will ever see. Hence, they attract lightning. When the Celts observed this phenomenon, they believed it was a divine message from the gods commanding them to worship these trees.

"*Daur*" is the Gaelic word for "Oak," which the English word door originates from. This stemmed from the belief that the sacred trees are gateways to another world. In fact, the Celts believed that if they slept under an oak tree, they might wake up in the realm of spirits.

The Celts associated the heart of an oak tree with fertility. They also believed that inside each oak tree lies the secrets and wisdom of the universe.

Since the Druids' name is derived from the Gaelic word for oak, they were considered the guardians of the gateway to the otherworld and experts in tree magic.

Crann Bethadh

Like the Norse, the Celts had a term for the Tree of Life, called "Crann Bethadh" in Gaelic, meaning "The feeding tree." Whenever they moved to a new town or built new settlements, the first thing the Celt did was plant an oak tree to guarantee abundance and prosperity and honor the Tree of Life.

All oak trees in ancient Ireland represented this sacred symbol. It was not thought of to build a town without this majestic tree standing tall and protecting the lands. During wartime, soldiers would cut down their enemies' Crann Bethadh. They believed this would weaken their defenses and make them vulnerable and easy to defeat. In fact, they would often celebrate when they cut down their adversaries' Tree of Life because they knew their enemies would lose the war without its support.

The Main Parts of the Tree of Life

If you look at an illustration of the Tree of Life, you will notice that the branches and roots are long and in perfect symmetry, with both mirroring one another to reflect balance and harmony. This depiction isn't random. It holds a deeper meaning behind it. The long branches that reach up to the sky and the roots that stretch deep under the ground symbolize the connection between the mind and the body, the spiritual and the physical, and heaven and Earth.

The Celts were impressed by the Tree of Life's strong root system. They would observe the size and weight of the oak tree and wonder how its roots managed to carry and support something that huge. As a result, the Tree of Life became a symbol of strength. To this day, people look at it in awe of its power. Although many other Celtic symbols reflect strength, none matches the majesty of the Tree of Life.

Many ancient Irish symbols include the Celtic knot, a looped knot pattern with no beginning or end. In other words, it is infinite, which represents eternal life. The knot on the Tree of Life signifies this never-ending life cycle.

Although there are many designs of the Tree of Life, it is always shown as a tree with multiple roots and branches spread above.

Interpretations of the Main Parts of the Tree of Life

- **Roots:** The roots symbolize the connection to the earth and physical existence. They represent the foundation of life and the significance of staying grounded in one's origins. The roots also symbolize the connection to the past and the wisdom of the elderly. They also represent the origin of one's family, like the ancestors or grandparents.

- **Trunk:** The trunk symbolizes the body and physical strength. It represents the ability to stand tall and weather the storms of life. It also symbolizes the connection between the spiritual world and the material world. It also represents the parents as they act as a link between the roots and the leaves. The trunk of the tree exists on Earth.
- **Branches:** The branches represent growth and expansion. They symbolize the potential for personal and spiritual growth and the ability to reach the heavens. The branches also represent the eternal life of the human soul.
- **Leaves:** The leaves symbolize abundance, fertility, and renewal, as well as the cycles of life and death that are part of the natural world. They also represent the offspring of a family.

The Tree of Life Symbolism

There are various interpretations of this ancient Celtic symbol. Since there aren't many records about the Celts or how they used to live their lives, scholars researched and analyzed the little information they have to develop these explanations. Since nothing is concrete, you can come up with your own interpretations. The tree can mean something different to many people depending on how it makes you feel.

The meaning behind the Tree of Life has also changed since the time of the Celts. However, one interpretation remains the same – that it represents the circle of life.

Immortality

The oak tree is one of the longest-living trees in the world, as it can live for six hundred or even one thousand years. When the tree roots and begins to die, its acorn seeds can grow into a large oak tree. Interestingly, this is the perfect representation of the circle of life. This also led the Celts to believe that the oak tree was immortal, while others believed it was their reincarnated ancestors.

Spiritual Connection

The circles found in many illustrations on the Tree of Life symbolize inclusion and connection. The tree also represents the connection between the physical and spiritual realms, the bridge between heaven and Earth. This shows that all living beings in the heavens and on Earth are linked together through the Tree of Life.

Rebirth and Change

One can tell the seasons are changing by observing the trees. In the fall, their leaves turn yellow; in the spring, their flowers bloom, and the leaves are full of life. However, the trees don't wither and die when the weather changes. They remain strong and adapt to change and keep growing.

The leaves falling in winter and growing in spring represent rebirth and human life. Even though you experience changes all the time, whether negative or positive, you keep growing and learn to endure and embrace whatever life has to offer.

Wisdom and Strength

Wisdom has always been associated with old age. Hence, oak trees became a symbol of wisdom and strength among the Celts. They watched this tree standing tall for centuries against thunder, rain, storms, and constant attacks from animals and human beings.

The Celts believed that since the oak trees spent more time on Earth than any other human, they had seen many things in this world and endured adversities by being exposed to tough weather conditions. They became a symbol of knowledge and endurance.

Family

The Tree of Life doesn't only symbolize the link between heaven and Earth but also family connections. There is a reason people often use the term family tree when they talk about their ancestors. The branches represent old family members and all the children who have been born.

If you look at your family tree, you will see pictures of your departed ancestors and your family's new members. This symbolizes the circle of life, with one life ending and another beginning.

Growth

Since trees live for centuries, they grow slowly throughout hundreds of years. The oak tree began its life as a small seed that grew over time into a large tree. The Tree of Life can represent growth and how human beings keep growing and changing until the end of their lives.

Rituals and Celebrations

Trees played a big role in the Druids' rituals and Celtic festivals and celebrations. For instance, to celebrate Beltane, the Celts would decorate a tree with flowers and ribbons to symbolize the Crann Bethadh and dance around it. During Samhain, they would gather around oak trees and pray to their ancestors.

The Tree of Life in Modern Times

Many Irish people still hold on to their ancestors' beliefs. If you visit Ireland, you will see how they incorporate ancient symbols in many designs. The Tree of Life will always be popular and special among Irish people of all ages. Some even get it tattooed on their body.

It is also one of the most common designs engraved on Irish urns since it shows that death isn't the end. It is a reminder that your loved ones aren't gone forever; they will be reborn. On the surface, the Crann Bethadh looks like a regular tree, but when you learn its true meaning, it can provide comfort. Death isn't something to be feared but merely a chapter in one's ongoing cycle of life. In some ancient cultures, funerals were happy events because they knew that the person would either be reincarnated or spend eternity in the otherworld.

Many cultures and religions believed in the Tree of Life before the Celts. It was a popular concept for which many people assigned meaning, legend, and beliefs. They believed that the Tree of Life was powerful and held the universe together and that the world would cease to exist without it.

All ancient cultures needed the concept of the Tree of Life. They wanted something bigger than them to represent the cycle of life and remind them that death wasn't the end. The Celts created this symbol to connect them to all the things that were out of their reach, like the heavens, the spirit realm, and their departed ancestors. The Tree of Life provided them with comfort that the universe was safe and in good hands.

The Celts and the Druids held trees in very high regard. When reading about their history, you will find that they played a big role in their daily lives, religious practices, and spirituality.

Looking around in nature, you will find that nothing is more powerful or majestic than trees. They manage to stand tall and remain strong no matter what the forces of nature throw at them. The Celts found them inspiring. If you spend some time in nature too and reflect on these magnificent plants, you will be moved by them as well.

Chapter 8: Animals as Celtic Symbols

Animals influenced numerous parts of ancient Celtic life. They shaped their religion, society, warfare, economics, art, and literature. This chapter delves into the role that animals played in Celtic mythology and spirituality. By reading it, you'll understand what animism is and its significance in ancient Celtic society. You'll find out how the ancient Celts approached and interacted with animals and come across plenty of interesting and informative tales of animal-related deities in the Celtic pantheon.

Animists are able to connect with nature spiritually and mystically.
https://www.pexels.com/photo/anonymous-person-standing-on-footpath-in-autumn-6272345/

What Is Animism?

There's a common misconception that animism is a religion. While animism is deeply tied to the world of spirituality, it is a culture-specific outlook on the universe. Animists believe that there is another world where spirits reside. According to this belief, spirits can meddle with human affairs, offer protection and guidance, or harm people. Animism is the belief that everything in nature, such as plants, animals, rocks, and bodies of water, has a spirit.

Animists have a unique way of experiencing the world. They know how to connect with nature by understanding the energetic frequencies that connect everything. Since animists have higher energetic vibrations and are tuned into the universe's energies, they have higher levels of consciousness. This enriches their spiritual endeavors and makes them more responsive to the natural and spiritual worlds. Animists understand that the otherworldly is interconnected with the terrestrial.

Ancient Celts and Animism

Animism was interwoven into the ancient Celtic tradition because, at the time, the world was predominantly based on nature and all things natural. Wild animals roamed freely, and humans developed a forest culture. They prayed to the oak trees, lived in mountains and forests, sought shade beneath the trees, and hunted and gathered for sustenance. They thrived on agriculture and based their calendar and festivities on the sun and agronomy. It goes without saying that the ancient Celts were a lot more connected to nature than the humans of the modern-day world.

The ancient Celts relied on natural resources to survive, which is why they prayed fervently to their gods for abundant harvests, fertile soil, and good weather. They believed they must give back to the world and the deities to reap the rewards of Earth, which is why they lived harmoniously and deeply connected to nature. They performed rituals, made offerings, and lived conscientiously to play their part in the universe.

Ancient Celts believed everything in nature was protected by a spirit guardian. They also thought that animals were the messengers of the deities. Some accounts suggest that ancient Celts believed that some of the deities manifested in the form of animals, while others claim that they revered nature without necessarily thinking that the deities took the form of animals. Regardless of the relationship between animals and deities, springs, hills, caves, and rivers, along with other elements of nature, were considered sacred.

The Celts held rituals and prayers in certain locations in nature because they believed they served as a portal to the spiritual realm. They set up shrines and places of worship close to groves of trees. This is where they held their social and spiritual meetings and called on the magical powers of the oaks for help and advice. The ancient Celts had secret groves of trees that they called the *nemeta*. They believed that these represented the unity between the earth and the heavens. The roots symbolized the Earth, and the branches embodied the sky.

Ancient Celts also believed celestial bodies, the weather, and other phenomena like storms and tsunamis were living beings. To ensure that the sun continues to shine, rain pours at adequate levels, and the sea stays neither too calm nor too angry, they had to appease and acknowledge these entities. The Celts were particularly concerned with thunder, seen in the many depictions of this phenomenon. To underscore the significance of thunder, the Celts worshipped Taranis, who was not only the god of thunder but was the personification of the occurrence itself.

What They Learned from Animals

The Celts believed they had a lot to learn from animals. Even though animals have their own languages, brains, and psyches, they are still intertwined with nature. Animals are fully present and aware of their surroundings when they are in nature. Animists closely interpret animal behavior and believe they can receive messages from the universe or higher powers through them or see omens in changes in their behaviors. Deities that share similar characteristics with certain animals were often named after them. *Epona*, the goddess of fertility and the protector of the equine, means "horse," and the Celtic bear goddess' name, Artio, also means "bear."

Ancient Celts found at least a few traits to admire about nearly every animal. They were certain that animals were blessed with a unique presence that humans could never fulfill, as well as traits and abilities that humans lacked. They knew the only ethical way to benefit and learn from these abilities was to honor animals and approach them with humility and respect.

Animals in Celtic Mythology

The Tale of the Cailleach

One Scottish Celtic myth revolved around a storm hag. Cailleach, the hag, embodied the force of nature and was responsible for triggering the first snowfall of the season. The crone was usually illustrated wearing a drab, enormous plaid cloak. She had a ghastly blue face and long, white hair. Being the hag deity of winter, Cailleach's hair carried speckles of frost. The Celts believed she had one eye in the middle of her forehead, signifying her ability to see everything that happens in all the realms. This was a characteristic shared by all omnipresent deities.

The Gaelic term "*Cailleach*" is derived from the word "pallium" in Latin, which translates to "veil." The ancient Celts may have chosen the name "veiled one" to refer to the crone deity to highlight her mysterious essence. Cailleach, however, is now loosely interpreted as the "old wife."

Legend says Cailleach went to a strait near the coast to wash her plaid. The tartan cloak was too huge and heavy that it stirred up a raging storm. The Gulf of Corryvreckan, the strait she was at, is known today for being one of the largest whirlpools on Earth. The term "*Corryvreckan*" translates to "cauldron of the plaid."

The crone's cloak became as white as snow and draped over the entire country during winter. Celtic animists believe Cailleach is the Scottish pantheon's most powerful deity. At the time, the winter was so long and harsh that people had to approach and acknowledge it courteously. Deities in other parts of the world, like Greece, were known for their beauty and what were regarded as ideal features at the time. This is why many people don't understand why anyone would worship a crone.

With little technology and nowhere to hide from the scorching heat of summer, freezing winters, wild animals, and other natural phenomena, ancient Celts understood that nature was unexpected, unsparing, and terrifying. Cailleach embodied this obscure, scary aspect of nature and was highly venerated for it.

Robert I and the Spider

The king of Scotland at the time, Robert I, fled to the Western Isles of Scotland after his army was conquered in war. He found a secluded cave in the isles, where he sought refuge and carefully curated a plan. Spending at least a few months there, the king often occupied himself by watching a spider as it meticulously built its web.

After Robert I, the king of Scotland, was defeated in battle, he sought refuge in the Western Isles of the nation. He ended up staying in a cave for a few months as he planned his next step. According to legend, the king watched a spider painstakingly build a web. Even though the average spider takes around 60 minutes to construct its shelter, the weather made the process particularly difficult for this arachnid.

Storms took the web apart each time the spider created it. The little creature, however, didn't give up. It kept rebuilding the web until it finally succeeded. Having been raised in an animist society, Robert I learned a lot from the spider. The message was clear: he needed to tackle what was in front of him without giving up, and this message needed to be spread to everyone.

Animism and Hunting

Even though ancient Celts revered animals, they still had to hunt for sustenance. They still approached their prey with honor and respect because they believed their lives depended on these animals' lives and deaths. They believed hunting was a venerated activity, and they couldn't take the lives of the hunted without the blessing of the corresponding deities. They sometimes sacrificed domestic animals to the corresponding deities to earn their blessings.

They also believed that they weren't harming nature by killing animals. Even though they took something from nature, they gave it something in return. The bloodshed from dead animals was thought to contain necessary nutrients and revitalizing power. The sacred act of hunting was celebrated because it contributed to the growth of nature, the lives of hunters, and the people they fed.

The Legend of the Selkie

Ancient Celts believed that some spirits came from several worlds at once. The selkie, a mythological creature, was one of them. Scottish selkies were thought to be powerful enough to transform from their seal-like form into a human once they left the sea. There is a tale of a man who spotted a selkie while he was on the beach.

This selkie took the form of a beautiful woman. The man fell in love and decided to steal the seal skin she'd shed so she could stay human. He forced her to marry him and carry his children. She spent most of her time gazing at the sea, missing what had been her home. A few years later, the woman finally found her selkie skin and jumped into the ocean. She loved her children but still wanted to go home. Some versions of the tale recount that the selkie visits them every year.

The Cunning Kelpies

The Kelpie is another shapeshifting creature in Scottish mythology. The horse-like figure can take human form, but some accounts suggest that it keeps its hooves. Some researchers explain that the Christian beliefs surrounding Satan and hooves come from this. Kelpies are believed to inhibit the isolated rivers and areas of Scotland. Kelpies are mainly white or grey and have long, wet manes. They appear to their victims, somehow convincing them to get on. Once the human rides the kelpie, the pony takes off and drowns them in the water.

The Morrigan and Cu Chulainn

The Morrigan, the deity of war, is popularly known as the Triple Goddess. The deity could tell which warriors would die in battle before it was time to fight. Her predictions also allowed her to steer the war's outcome in her desired direction. She was able to shapeshift into a crow and flew over battlegrounds. Crows are generally believed to be a bad omen, which is why her presence either struck fear into the nerves of warriors or motivated them to fight harder.

The goddess fell in love with Cu Chulainn, a heroic warrior who was half human and half divine. Known for her beauty, the Morrigan could seduce the most powerful of men. However, her tricks didn't work on Cu Chulainn when she approached him before he went to war. He turned her down, which drove her to seek revenge.

Mid-battle, the goddess decided to shapeshift into an eel, swim up to the warrior hero, and trip him. Cu Chulainn naturally punched the animal away and continued to fight. The deity once again transformed into a gigantic wolf. She ran at him, pushing cattle toward the hero. Once again, he fought back and threw a stone into the wolf's eye. The Morrigan went temporarily blind but shifted into a cow for one last time. She gathered a herd of cows and moved toward Cu Chulainn.

He, however, quickly moved out of the herd's way and threw another stone at the Morrigan. This time, the stone hit and broke her leg. Hurt enough, the goddess decided to accept defeat. After the warrior hero won the battle, he met an old woman on his way back to the base. The lady was milking a cow, but Cu Chulainn was too tired to notice her leg and eye injuries. Not recognizing that she was the Morrigan, he stopped right in front of the woman and sparked a conversation with her.

The woman, who appeared gentle and harmless, offered Cu Chulainn a glass of milk which he accepted. He downed the entire glass, but little did he know that drinking the milk would heal the Morrigan and give her strength. The Morrigan didn't care to fight Cu Chulainn anymore. Tricking him into healing her was revenge enough for her.

The warrior hero and the goddess crossed paths once again right before he died. Cu Chulainn was heading to another battle when he saw a woman scrubbing blood off the armor. He knew that this sight was a very bad omen when he was about to face an enemy. Cu Chulainn continued walking toward the battlefield regardless.

This battle, just as he anticipated, was the end of Cu Chulainn. He was severely wounded but still managed to fight until his last breath. The hero tied himself to a boulder, hoping to scare any enemies passing by. The Morrigan, in the form of a cross, rested on his shoulder until he passed away peacefully.

Cernunnos the Antlered God

Cernunnos was a deity who appeared in half human half stag form. He was brought into the world during the winter solstice, known as the year's darkest day. Even though he was associated with the harsh, dreary winter, the deity married Beltane, the goddess of spring. However, their happiness wasn't long-lasting because he died six months later on the summer solstice. The Celts believed him to be a wise teacher, which is why they depicted him cross-legged.

Cernunnos was the deity of the underworld, animals, prosperity, and fertility. Very little about the antlered god is known, further reinforcing his mysterious facade. No mythological tales emerged about him, so most of what is known about him is from Celtic iconography. His most notable depiction shows him carrying a serpent and a torc, surrounded by a number of animals – like a raven, dog, and stag. Cernunnos ruled over nature and animals. Researchers suggest that ancient Celts brought the deity offerings of elk, snakes, wolves, and other animals to thank them for creating peace between enemies. He was an esteemed protector and wise man among the tribes.

Another image portrays the deity as a bald man with the ears of a stag. His bald head is an allusion to eldership and wisdom. His antlers are thought to be a reflection of his humility and groundedness. The torque reflects his powerful status and ability to conquer enemies and offer courage and protection to those needing them.

The belief that he was born on the winter solstice and died on the summer solstice suggests that he's associated with heightened energy levels, incredible spiritual experiences, and augmentation. However, since he died just inside the second half of the agricultural cycle, the antlered god wasn't blessed with the introspective traits associated with the harvesting season. It also signifies his lack of "completeness" as a symbol of masculinity and potency. Cernunnos' marriage to Beltane, however, brought some balance into his life.

The Significance of the Stag

The stag is a symbol of wisdom and knowledge in Celtic traditions. This animal is also associated with the natural cycle of life. It symbolizes life, death, and rebirth since it regrows a new set of antlers every year. White stags are also particularly spiritually significant because they represent purity. They're related to divine energies and spiritual enlightenment.

Stags are powerful animals, which makes them symbols of masculinity, motivation, and vitality. Many spiritual individuals believe that crossing paths with a stag serves as a reminder of one's inner strength and perseverance. These are the spirit animals to turn to or animals to observe whenever you feel stuck in life.

Stags are naturally inclined to live in solitude, so animists believe they can learn how to be independent and self-reliant from them. Stags remind people that alone time is necessary to reflect and experience mental, emotional, and spiritual growth.

The stag is believed to be the protector of the other animals and is therefore seen as the king of the forest. Leadership, guardianship, and guidance are among a few of this animal's qualities, which is why deities associated with it, such as Cernunnos, take on significant roles in their society. The stag also bridges between terrestrial and heavenly matters, as well as the masculine and the physical. It brings harmony and balance into the world, which is why ancient Celts also believed it to be a spiritual messenger. Encountering a stag meant that they needed to become more spiritually involved or be more receptive to signs from the divine.

Regardless of whether you believe in Celtic mythology and folklore, you can learn a lot from the ancient Celts. Observing how animals interact with nature, treating them with respect, and understanding their role in the world can enrich your spiritual experience and heighten your consciousness. The next time you see a spider spinning its web, or a seal moving toward the shore, ask yourself how an animist or ancient Celt would have reflected on the occurrence.

Chapter 9: Celtic Divination

Divination is a method of seeking knowledge about unknown events from the future. The ancient Celts used divination to uncover what lies beneath the surface of what was happening around them and how it connected with the universe. The most widespread Celtic divination method involves the Ogham alphabet, which has become a popular prophecy tool in modern times but was not well documented in ancient times. Different techniques for Ogham divination were passed down through generations, and it's unknown which one the ancient Celts considered the most accurate. The Ogham divination method is most commonly used in Ireland, from where the Ogham letters are believed to originate.

The Celts decipher Ogham symbols to know more about their future.
https://www.pexels.com/photo/anonymous-female-soothsayers-with-crystal-ball-and-tarot-card-during-divination-session-6944350/

The Ogham methodology works just like any other divination tool. After researching it and familiarizing themselves with the method, the practitioner gets comfortable handling it regularly. Then, they can ask questions about events, situations, people, and outcomes they're interested in. The inquiry can be made to the deities, the Spirit of Ogham, and spiritual guides with whom one wants to connect or work. You can present your question verbally or write them down and incorporate either method into your divination rituals. You can ask any question you want, but beginners are advised to keep their inquiries simple. By asking one simple question at a time, you can focus on it and the answer much better. Once you practice this for a while, you can start making more complex inquiries during divination.

Using Ogham divination is a great way to learn to understand yourself – to see how your life unfolds and understand why – and, if needed, make changes to achieve different results. In ancient times, Celts used this tool to ensure a plentiful harvest, favorable endings in battle, and similar feats. The Ogham divination is mentioned in several Irish poems, including the Bríatharogaim (Morainn mac Moín, Maic ind Óc, and Con Culainn), all of which were commonly used as divinatory insights by the Old Irish. Some modern practitioners still use these texts as poetic tools for memorizing the names of the letters of the Ogham alphabet and the spiritual meanings attached to them.

Nowadays, practitioners use Ogham to figure out how to move forward in life – by changing certain aspects of it. It's a particularly popular method among Druids, who undergo lengthy training to gain experience in deciphering complex spiritual messages they receive from deities and spirit guides. Of course, you don't have to practice it for years as they do, but you'll still need to be patient if you're a complete beginner. Without any knowledge of divination and how to interpret the messages, it will take some time to learn how to do this. You can start by choosing a part of your life you want to explore and focus on it while practicing.

Ogham divination relies on a set of 25 symbols, each associated with the letters of the ancient Irish Gaelic writings. Each Ogham symbol denotes a letter's name related to the others within its Aicme (grouping). The symbols hold the key to the layered and deep-seated meanings you can apply when interpreting the answers to your questions. Depending on the context, each letter can have a different symbolism.

According to the Neo-Pagans, and other New Age practitioners, Ogham divination hails from a version of the Celtic Tree Oracle and is based on the Celtic Tree Calendar. Older sources claim that this is inaccurate. They assert that there is much more to the Ogham than its connection to tree lore, which New Age practitioners typically focus on. The tree-based philosophy is featured in the Book White Goddess, written by Robert Graves, a prominent English poet, critic, and historical novelist. Those who base their work on ancient Celtic and Druidic traditions see tree associations as a necessary part of understanding prophetic messages but do not rely exclusively on them. They combine it with other divination methods or spiritual work.

Casting and Reading Ogham Symbols

Traditionally, the Ogham symbols are etched into wooden staves. The staves are then used during divination rituals. However, since they're just simple lines anyone can replicate, the symbols can be inscribed and even written on any surface. You can simply pen them on paper, carve them into small wooden sticks to create your own set or buy them in the most convenient form.

Ogham symbols are read from the bottom up. Traditional methods for casting the staves include drawing them from a bag, throwing them onto a cloth, or arranging them in a specific pattern.

The drawing method is typically recommended for beginners. Here is how to do it:

1. Fill a bag with your staves – you can also use a box, hat, or whatever vessel is convenient for you.
2. Pick one stave and get it out from the vessel without looking at it.
3. Focus on your intention, ask a question, and look at the symbol. Think about what it means to you. You can also consult the predefined meanings of the symbols.
4. When you feel you've received an answer, complete your reading by putting the staves away.
5. If you didn't get an answer or don't know how to interpret it, don't worry. This is common for novices and just means you have to practice.

6. Once you get the gist of the practice, you can start picking three staves out from the vessel and following the same steps shown above. These are avenues to learn about past, present, and future outcomes.

Choosing and casting several staves by laying them out on a piece of cloth is another easy-to-do method. Here is how to execute it:

1. Choose the number of symbols you want to interpret. Depending on your experience and the nature of the information you seek, this can vary from three to six to nine.
2. Lay a piece of cloth in front of you. Do this in a quiet place where you won't be disturbed.
3. Reach into the container with the staves and start getting them out. Throw them down in front of you one by one.
4. As you take each stave into your hands, think about your intention and the questions you want to ask. Take a few moments to connect your intention with each stave.
5. Take a few additional moments to look at them when they're all in front of you and contemplate their meanings.
6. When ready, think about how the symbols you see can answer your question or queries.

Creating a spread requires more experience and is recommended for those who have mastered the first two techniques. Here is how to do it:

1. Consider what you want to learn during the reading. For example, you can explore past, present and future outcomes, spiritual, emotional, and physical aspects of your life, or your connections to a deity, ancestors, and spirits.
2. Draw three staves from your vessel and lay them out in front of you. Focus on the trio of aspects you've chosen to explore.
3. For example, if you picked the time aspects, the first stave will give your answers about past events affecting your outcome, the second one about the present, and the third about what you can expect in the future.
4. Ruminate on the meanings of the staves in front of you. When you have your answers, finish the ritual.

While the one-stave method usually relies on the upright meaning of the symbols, if you're going to use any other technique, consider the staves' reverse symbolism too. Another helpful tip is always to have an open mind when making a prophetic inquiry and waiting for an answer. Consider various options and avoid asking questions that can be answered with a "yes" or a "no." Remember, there are no right and wrong answers either. While the explanation you get could make sense to you right away, if you keep listening to your intuition, it will soon become much clearer.

Cultivating Your Relationship with the Symbols

The best part of Ogham divination is that you can cultivate a personal relationship with the symbols and their energies. This practice relies on skills that allow you to engage with the physical, emotional, spiritual, and mental parts of yourself. Naturally, you'll need discipline and patience, but the results will be all the more rewarding. You'll unlock your natural potential, connect with your past, present, and future and reclaim balance and harmony in your life. You'll learn how you fit into this universe, reveal your purpose, and learn about your heritage (if you're interested in exploring a potential Celtic ancestry).

To build a connection with the symbols, you must also engage with two realms of Celtic cosmology, the Otherworld and the real world. This will give you access to information hidden from most people – and use this knowledge to improve your life and the life of those around you. Below are some of the best ways to cultivate your relationship with Ogham symbols.

Developing Deeper Awareness and Mindfulness through Meditation

A great way to form a connection to the symbols is by developing and enhancing your awareness and mindfulness skills. Meditation is a mindfulness technique designed to improve focus, which is the first step in gaining awareness of yourself and your surroundings. When you meditate, you start noticing a powerful sense of presence – the presence of your energies. You're opening up to the possibility of encountering and embracing new connections and relationships.

Meditation also helps you see what truly matters and focuses your energy on manifesting your intention. Most of the time, this means taking actions that will cause changes. Meditation can help you reach insights about your inner world, so you can make more informed choices.

Implementing Ogham Practices in Your Life

Regular Ogham rituals and practices are fundamental to improving your spiritual and mental health, which, in turn, will help you form stronger connections with the Spirit of Ogham and the deities and guards you choose to work with. A great way to start introducing Ogham practices into your daily life is by observing the Moon while holding the symbols. As you do this day after day, you start feeling the changes in your energy and the energies of the signs. Patterns will emerge, and a cyclical alignment will begin. It's a good idea to keep a record of what you encounter to see how your connection with the symbols develops over time.

Besides drawing an Ogham symbol every day, you can begin doing small daily rituals like setting intentions, holding the staves in your hand as you meditate, or dedicating time to silently contemplate the staves' meanings. Consciously connecting with the symbols daily is a fantastic way to improve focus, eliminate distractions and raise your awareness. You'll feel more in tune with yourself, the symbols, and the realms in Celtic cosmology.

Opening Yourself Up to Natural Energies

To connect with the symbols, you must learn how to embrace the natural energies around you. Opening up to these energies will allow you to work with any spiritual tools, including Ogham divination. Take a few minutes daily to spend time with the staves and fully feel their energy. They can be powerful, but don't be afraid or discouraged. Invite them into your life. Do this in the open, where you can feel closer to the natural world. Just sit in a secluded spot in nature and take in everything around you – the scents, the images, the sounds, and everything you notice about your surroundings. Alternatively, you can spend time in liminal spaces where you can also be close to the Otherworld. It's critical to explore its energies too. The spirits can be great allies in a divination practice.

Interpreting Ogham Readings

Besides being a powerful divination tool, Ogham symbols represent a unique mixture of mystical and mundane wisdom, which resonate within everyone. Their meanings are deeply connected with the natural cycles of life and the traditions of the ancient Celts. Make sure you consider this when learning how to interpret Ogham readings.

Here are a few other factors to consider when interpreting the symbols:
- Each symbol is associated with a sacred tree but can have many other metaphorical meanings you can connect to spiritually.
- The vast knowledge the symbols convey guarantees that you'll take the time to slow down. You'll need time to learn their unique meanings.
- You can interpret Ogham symbols like runes and Tarot cards by assigning an intention and question to them and then choosing how to present them.
- One-stave and three-stave readings work best for beginners because they're simple enough to interpret.

Here is an example of how to do this in practice:
1. In the morning, form a question you want to be answered. For example, you can ask something like:

   "What should I do to make the best out of this day?"
2. Focusing on the question, take three staves out of their bag or box. Lay them side by side.
3. The one on the left will provide information about yourself, the one in the middle shows events and situations you'll encounter during the day, and the one on the right shows you the outcome.
4. Look at the symbols to see their position and possible meaning. Are any of them reversed? If yes, this could indicate that something is contrary to what you would like it to be.

Working with the Symbols

There are numerous ways to work with Ogham symbols. For example, you can incorporate them into meditation or combine them with other forms of divination. If you choose the latter, you can, for instance, choose dreamwork or journeying. Dream prophecy is recommended for beginners who struggle with working out and interpreting messages while awake. To do this, you only need to take a stave (or three) and ask the question you want answered before going to sleep. The resolution will come in your dreams. Keep a piece of paper on your nightstand. You should record the messages you've obtained as soon as you wake up.

Ogham Meditation

When working with Ogham, a meditation technique that relies on the ancient Tree Lore can give much better insight. Channeling tree energy while meditating enables you to become even more familiar with the spiritual energies around you, including the ones in the symbols. Although the instructions will ask you to start your circle from the North, feel free to begin with the direction that resonates with you. Some practitioners prefer to start from the East, while others will alternate approaches depending on the seasons.

Tools you'll need:

- Wooden staves – or wands. Some practitioners prefer using trees associated with the Ogham alphabet. However, you can use the staves that symbolize them too.
- One large candle
- Incense
- A small container, preferably glass or ceramic – for the incense
- A cup of wine, beer, or mead
- Any object you want to use to improve focus
- Working surface – a portable altar or a small table you've cleared off
- A chair or cushion – depending on where you'll be sitting
- Music or sounds to meditate – optional
- Athame – optional
- Ritual clothing or jewelry, talismans – optional
- Four smaller candles represent the four cardinal directions

Instructions:

1. Choose the best place to meditate. If you're conducting the ritual outdoors, find a secluded natural environment. If you're meditating indoors, ensure that nothing and no one will disturb you.
2. Set an intention for your meditation ritual. It will help you remain focused.
3. Choose the trees with the energy you want to channel. For example, for strength and growth, you'll need oak. For balance and empathy, use holly. Whereas for protection and warding off

negative energies, it's best to work with hawthorn.

4. You can use one wand or stave or different ones with similar energies to enhance a particular intention. Avoid channeling the essence of more than three trees at a time. Beginners are advised to use only one tree.

5. Arrange the four smaller candles so they're placed on the East, West, North, and South to complete a sacred circle. It will help you channel and balance the energies within the circle.

6. Set up a table or portable altar in the middle of the circle. Place the large candle, the wands or staves, the incense, and the item for focus on the table or altar.

7. Once all the items are on the table, light your incense and the candle while focusing on your intention. If you wish, start the meditation music or sound recording.

8. When you're ready to begin the ritual, take a deep breath and face North. Continuing breathing deeply, welcome the element of the Earth and the essence of the tree you're trying to channel. Think about the properties of this tree and express your respect for them silently or out loud.

9. Moving clockwise, repeat the step from above in the direction of East, South, and West, respectively. While doing this, touch the stave or wand a couple of times to empower your physical connection with the tree.

10. If you're using an athame, point it in the direction you're facing each time. Once you've greeted the tree in the last direction, you've completed your sacred circle.

11. Depending on your beliefs and practices, you can now invite and welcome any spiritual guide or deity into the circle.

12. Sit in front of your table or portable altar. Once again, you can choose which direction you want to face. Just make sure you're comfortable, so you can focus on your intention and the objects you'll use to manifest it.

13. Take a few moments to observe the candle, the staves or wands, and any other items you use for focus.

14. When you have become familiar and connected with the latter, take a sip from the cup. Feel the liquid travel through you, relaxing your mind, body, and spirit.

15. Use a familiar meditation technique for further relaxation. For example, you can choose to let your eyelids drop slowly while breathing deeply and focus on how this makes you feel. Or you can gaze into the candle while breathing deeply – until you relax and reach a deeper stage of consciousness.
16. Once you're in a deep meditation state, you'll be ready to explore the realms of wisdom, divination, and inspiration. Remain in this state for as long as you desire.
17. When your meditation is complete, you'll need to close the ritual. Begin by facing West, thank the element of water and the tree energy for their assistance, and bid them farewell.
18. If you've summoned any spiritual guides or deities, send a quick prayer of gratitude to them as well.
19. Move anti-clockwise towards the South, East, and North. Once again, the direction to start with is optional, but make sure to move anti-clockwise from whichever direction you begin dismantling the ritual.
20. Extinguish the incense and the candles, remove the rest of the items from the table, and put away the stave or wand you used. Alternatively, you can leave the circle active by leaving everything on the table but snuffing out the candles.
21. When you're ready, put everything away.

Bonus: Tree Meditations

Trees have been worshiped throughout history by many cultures, but they've always held a special place of reverence in Celtic traditions. Trees are universally regarded as a symbol of wisdom and life, as they represent a primordial bond that transcends the boundaries of time and civilization. As you've learned in this book, trees have a special significance in Celtic symbolism due to the Celt's close affinity to the natural world. Whether you consider the Celtic Tree calendar being linked with sacred trees or the Ogham script, where each letter has been associated with a particular tree, you'll see trees' importance everywhere in Celtic culture. In fact, the Celts recognized the significance of trees very early on and considered them to be the central axis of their mythology. To them, trees were not merely a source of sustenance, shelter, and warmth but nature's pure essence.

Buddha practicing tree meditation.
Thomas Nordwest, CC BY-SA 4.0 <https://creativecommons.org/licenses/by-sa/4.0>, via Wikimedia Commons: https://commons.wikimedia.org/wiki/File:Buddha_in_Meditation_2023-05-11-22.jpg

Within the Celtic society, the Druids were believed to have the unique ability to decipher the subtle messages conveyed by Mother Nature. Through these messages, they sought to communicate and interact with the gods and goddesses and even invoke their presence using the ancient sentinels of the forests - the trees. The Celts believed that trees acted as a link between realms in a physical and divine sense. They believed each part of the tree symbolized a different realm, each connected to the other. The trunk of the tree represents the material world, providing people with food, safety, and shelter. The roots went deep into the soil and symbolized the realm of dreams and the latent wisdom of Earth. Finally, the crown and branches of the tree reach skywards, swayed by the wind, which symbolizes the divine plane of consciousness.

The significance of trees in Celtic culture is further proven by the fact that the Druids, who were the highest class among the Celtic people, made their homes among these majestic beings. They rarely ventured into the confines of the villages and instead preferred to stay on the outskirts near the sacred groves where they could be in complete harmony with the trees. Celtic tree meditations are among the most famous rituals of the Celtic culture and hold considerable reverence. Even today, many people choose to practice these guided meditations to connect with their higher consciousness and become harmonious with nature. This bonus chapter will give you a comprehensive list of guided meditations unique to each sacred tree revered in the Celtic world. So, prepare to immerse yourself in the profound wisdom of trees and experience the transformative power of tree meditations.

Birch Tree Meditation

Birch trees are capable of thriving in diverse environments, even in bare soil, and they usually grow in clusters. These ethereal trees are easy to spot due to their white and papery bark. This sturdy tree is not just useful for practical purposes like making furniture but is also very popular from a magical perspective. The outer white bark can be used in rituals to replace paper or parchment, while other parts of the tree are usually used for medicinal purposes. The Birch tree is considered to be one of the three sacred trees for the Druids. In Celtic symbolism, this tree is often called the Goddess Tree, which represents fertility, light, hope, regeneration, and new beginnings. Being a pioneer species, Birch trees have the unique ability to recolonize in case of an ecological disaster, like a forest fire. For this reason, this species is often compared to the Phoenix and linked to rebirth energy in a big way. Birch tree meditation is a wonderful way to enhance your spiritual understanding of

Celtic traditions while also gaining insight. If you're starting a new chapter in your life, practicing this meditation is the perfect way to do it.

- Tree meditation is most effective in the presence of the said tree in real time. However, if that's not possible, you can also keep a picture of the tree in front of your meditation space.
- Pick a comfortable position under the tree, or in your meditation space, with your legs crossed. Close your eyes, and take a few deep breaths to ground yourself.
- If you're indoors, a great way to mimic the natural environment is to put on some nature sounds like birds chirping, wind whistling, tree leaves falling, etc.
- Call upon the Birch tree spirit to join you in meditation. Visualize the presence of the Birch spirit standing or sitting beside you, emitting a white light.
- Set your intention by asking these questions, either out loud or silently:
  - Where in my life do I need an infusion of new energy?
  - Where do I need to regenerate?
  - What part of my life has a new chapter coming?
- Once you have finished asking these questions, open your mind and heart to any spiritual guidance you may receive. Be receptive and curious about any intuitions, impressions, or thoughts.
- Take your time in this receptive state and visualize the Birch spirit trying to communicate with you. Take deep, regular breaths, and you might feel a sense of clarity, inspiration, or subtle energy shifts.
- Once you feel you've gotten your guidance, express gratitude to the Birch spirit for joining you in the meditation and guiding you forward.
- Finally, open your eyes, and take a moment to note any impressions, messages, or insights you received during the meditation session.
- Over the next few days, reflect on the messages you've received while keeping in mind patterns the Birch tree is associated with.

- Also, keep your eyes open for any Birch trees that appear unexpectedly in your surroundings.

Rowan Tree Meditation

The Rowan tree is powerful, with beautiful foliage and ruddy berries. This tree has been associated with protection and magic since ancient times when Druids used to practice tree magic. The tree's bark has significant medicinal benefits and magical uses. Protective charms were frequently carved onto Rowan sticks and placed over windows and doorways to keep evil spirits out. Rune staves, wooden sticks with symbols carved on them, were usually created with Rowan wood. Even the berries that inhabit this tree have protective magic. When the berries are sliced in half, a little pentagram that is related to protective symbols is seen on the interior. The Rowan tree is a tree for all seasons and is especially sacred to most Earth religions. Ancient Celtic legends say Druids would get visions while staying in dedicated Rowan groves. Rowan meditation will help clear your mind, attune to nature, and view the world differently. Rowan is about creativity, intention setting, unconditional love, and astral travel.

- Play calming music that puts you into a dreamy, trance-like state. Get into a comfortable position, and close your eyes.
- Ground and center yourself and breathe into your heart. Inhale, pulling energy up from the earth, and exhale it out in all directions.
- Pull energy up from your crown chakra and breathe it out in all directions. Take a few moments to experience this breath.
- In your mind, travel to a place in nature where you feel peaceful. Visualize that it's winter, and you're dressed warmly.
- From the sky, your spirit horse, all white and mighty, arrives. Take a moment to look at your spirit horse, at the majestic power in its body.
- Imagine yourself mounting your spirit horse and setting off into the sky. Look down at the world from the sky and notice the perspective.
- Take a moment to feel the freedom of flight and let yourself really soar. As you fly high above the earth, your spirit horse will fly to the dimensions of the priestess of Rowan.

- Looking down, you see a landscape filled with beautiful Rowan trees, with their clusters of red and orange berries. You land safely between the trees.
- Dismount your horse and turn your attention to the beautiful grove of Rowan trees. Breathe in the wonderful forest sense, and you'll feel there's inspiration everywhere in this realm full of possibilities.
- Envision a beautiful priestess approaching you from a far-off distance; she comes close to you and places a crown made of Rowan leaves on your head.
- Seek her protective guidance, and she will become your ally. Take time to receive her offerings.
- Show her places in your body, mind, and soul that are distressing you. She will gladly lighten your load and give you inspiration. She will heal you.
- Agree to enlarge your belief system to include more and more of the mystery and magic of creation; connect these to the higher dimensions of love.
- Thank the priestess for her presence in the world. When you're ready, fly back to your world on your spirit horse.
- Take a moment to thank your spirit horse. Ground and center in this space and time. Stay here quietly for a moment and ponder the beauty of your experience!
- Upon returning, write your experiences down in a journal so you don't forget the details of what you felt during your journey.

Alder Tree Meditation

The Alder tree is associated with the spring equinox and symbolizes the evolving spirit. Like birch trees, Alder trees can withstand harsh conditions like swampy locations since their wood doesn't rot when wet. It really hardens when left to sit in water, which the Britons found useful while they were constructing fortresses in early Ireland. The city of Venice itself is said to be built on Alder wood. According to Celtic mythology, Alder trees are associated with the Otherworld, which is where spirits and deities reside. According to another legend, the Alder tree can be used by mediums who want to connect with humans no longer in their physical form. As a result, Druids used to sit in quiet meditation beneath Alder trees and even absorb the flower essence for this purpose.

- Close your eyes and take a few deep breaths to relax and focus. Sit under an Alder tree or in a solitary meditation space.
- Picture roots growing out of your feet and the base of your spine and plant them into the earth. Send them down through all the layers of the earth, branching in all directions.
- Send them down to the earth's center, where a big white ball of energy is located. Now picture this light traveling up through the roots, similar to how roots draw up moisture and sustenance from the earth.
- The energy flows up every root through all the layers of the earth up through the soles of your feet and tailbone. With every breath in, draw this energy up to your heart.
- And as you breathe out, move this energy from your heart down your arms and into your hands; feel the center of your palms get warm.
- With your inhalation, bring the energy back up your arms into your heart and exhale the energy further up through your body and out the crown of your head through your crown chakra.
- As you send this energy out, you observe the energy flowing through the branches going out of your head and shoulders. Send this energy up and up through the sky until it reaches the sun or the moon.
- Feel the energy coursing through your body and feel it energize you.
- Now picture yourself standing in a meadow of lush green grass, the sun is shining bright in the sky, and you feel its warmth and smile.
- You are at peace in the meadow; you see a beautiful creek lined with tall alder trees in the distance. You feel the tall grass swish around your legs.
- You move toward the row of trees and stand under their shade. Looking at the creek, you sense a balance of energy between the water's feminine energy and the trees' masculine energy.
- You feel calm, centered, and completely protected; you turn to face a tree, reach out a hand and place it on the trunk, and feel

the bark under your fingers.
- Give your greetings to the tree in whatever way you see fit. Thank the tree for the beautiful energy you feel here today.
- Now sit under the tree; you can even lean against it with your back to it but sit in a comfortable spot and close your eyes.
- Slow your breathing and feel yourself relax; push your awareness outside of yourself and sense the presence of the tree near you.
- Feel how both of your energies become one, a sense that there is no boundary as you merge. What do you feel, see, hear, or maybe smell?
- Once you feel you have made a strong connection with the alder tree, ask the tree a question you need help with or ask for its protective energy for whatever issues you're currently facing.
- Show your gratitude to the alder tree, and once you've received an answer, stand up, and move back into your plane of existence.
- Slowly open your eyes and ground yourself. Write down any insights you gained from the session.

Willow Tree Meditation

The Willow tree usually grows near water, and when nourished properly, it grows quite fast. This tree is representative of spiritual growth and knowledge and offers protection and healing. In folk medicine, the Willow tree has been used to treat various ailments like coughs, fevers, and other inflammatory conditions. Although many people confuse the Willow tree with the Weeping Willow, both trees are different, although resembling each other. Willow tree meditation is used to promote deep healing and help you release your emotional clutter.

- Find a comfortable place where you won't be disturbed for a while. Sit in a comfortable position and take a deep breath. Close your eyes.
- Slowly inhale and exhale. Connect with your environment by feeling the ground beneath you or the scents around you.
- Now visualize a majestic Willow tree in the heat of the summer. The trees are full of green and golden leaves, standing in a stunning field.

- Breathe the air in the field and feel the sun's warmth on your skin. Look at the beautiful droopy leaves of the tree.
- The wind blows them, so they swing gracefully. Watch the birds flying by and caressing the leaves at the branches of the willow.
- Now, think of any issues you're having in your life. Imagine that you pick up the problem and hang it on one of the trees. Let the problem take any physical form you want or no form at all.
- Think of any other problems and repeat the same process. Imagine hanging all your problems on the branches of different willow trees.
- Step about 20 feet back from the Willow trees. Notice how the wind blows the leaves and the problems as they hang on the branches.
- Allow some of the problems to be lifted by the wind and carried away; wave them goodbye as they float away. Take note of the problems that were carried away.
- Now, walk closer to the tree, and imagine that you can actually walk into the trunk of the tree. Feel the effortless weight of the branches and the wind blowing through your leaves.
- Feel that you, as the tree, are strong and that you can let every problem go. Even if some of the issues are still hanging on the branches.
- Feel the calm tranquility of the willow, letting go of your worries with each breeze. When you're ready, you can open your eyes and come back to your space.

Tree meditations have always held a significant place in Celtic spirituality. They provide a unique opportunity to connect with the wisdom and energy of trees, offering a sense of calm and grounding that is unmatched by any other form of meditation. By embracing tree meditations, you can tap into the timeless teachings of nature, fostering tranquility and deepening your understanding of your place in the world.

Conclusion

A single book is not enough to hold the vast knowledge of Celtic mythology, spirituality, and symbolism. Just the symbolism of Celtic culture could be discussed for thousands of pages. In any case, mythology, symbolism, and spirituality are all interconnected, and in order to understand one, it's crucial to understand the other, and so on. From the fascinating history of the Celts to the enigmatic wisdom of the Druids, Celtic lore and symbolism have captured hearts and minds worldwide. Scholars have been studying Celtic symbols in this culture for decades and are still doing so because of the vast meanings and interpretations of the unique and deeply powerful symbols.

What sets Celtic symbolism apart from any other language is that it's not simply ornamental or used for communicative purposes. It holds a deeper significance and wisdom waiting to be discovered. Whether it's the intricate knot work, the majestic animals, or the enigmatic spirals, each symbol has layers and layers of meanings and interpretations that beg for introspection. Take the Celtic Cross as an example, it seems like a simple symbol at first glance, but once you find out its context, the symbol transforms how you look at this world. It represents the interconnectedness of the spiritual and material world and how balance and harmony must be achieved within both. Or consider the Triskele, with its three spirals, symbolizing the eternal cycles of life, death, and rebirth. Each symbol acts as a mirror, reflecting one's life experiences and encouraging one to seek inspiration and a unique worldview.

It is simply not enough to just observe these symbols from a distance. The power of Celtic symbolism lies in its ability to guide and inspire you in parts of your life; simply considering these symbols and their associations as something from history or myth does not help you in any way. Only when you gain actual insight from it that you can apply to your life do you truly fulfill the purpose of these symbols. You must try to infuse your actions, thoughts, and intentions with the essence of these ancient teachings and embrace the deeper meaning behind each symbol. In addition to applying the teachings and interpretations of various symbols into your life, you could also try to integrate the Celtic culture through practical applications like engaging in rituals, practicing spiritual meditation, and immersing yourself in Celtic art and literature. All of these avenues push you toward a stronger connection with the Celts and their rich culture.

As this journey concludes, you should reflect on what you've learned. And continue your quest for knowledge and understanding. There are so many aspects and perspectives about Celtic symbolism and unlimited resources at your fingertips, so why not take this opportunity and learn more about the ancient wisdom of the Celts? May the wisdom of Celtic mythology, spirituality, and symbolism continue to inspire and empower you on your life's journey as you apply these ancient teachings to your own existence; may you find transformation, connection, and a deeper understanding of yourself and the world around you.

Here's another book by Mari Silva that you might like

Your Free Gift
(only available for a limited time)

Thanks for getting this book! If you want to learn more about various spirituality topics, then join Mari Silva's community and get a free guided meditation MP3 for awakening your third eye. This guided meditation mp3 is designed to open and strengthen ones third eye so you can experience a higher state of consciousness. Simply visit the link below the image to get started.

https://spiritualityspot.com/meditation

Or, Scan the QR code!

References

(N.d.-e). Ireland-calling.com. https://ireland-calling.com/celtic-mythology-elder-tree/

"The Kelpies": ancient myth in modern art. (n.d.). Artuk.org. https://artuk.org/learn/learning-resources/the-kelpies-ancient-myth-in-modern-art

A Celtic meditation that connects you with the earth--and the ancestors. - Beliefnet. (n.d.). Beliefnet.com. https://www.beliefnet.com/faiths/pagan-and-earth-based/2001/11/the-yew-tree-path-a-meditation.aspx

A Druid Ogham. (n.d.). A Druid Ogham. https://druidogham.wordpress.com/

Ancient Celtic Religion. (n.d.). Tutorialspoint.Com. https://www.tutorialspoint.com/ancient-celtic-religion

Asher, H. (2023, April 8). The moon as a calendar. An Darach Forest Therapy. https://silvotherapy.co.uk/articles/the-moon-as-a-calendar

Beltane. (2015, August 12). By Land, Sea, and Sky. https://thenewpagan.wordpress.com/beltane/

Bhagat, D. (n.d.). The origins and practices of: Samhain, día de los Muertos, and all saints day. Bpl.org. https://www.bpl.org/blogs/post/the-origins-and-practices-of-holidays-samhain-dia-de-los-muertos-and-all-saints-day/

Bot detection! (n.d.). Youglish.com. https://youglish.com/pronounce/yule/english/uk

Brethauer, A. (2021, April 8). Ogham Alphabet Meanings, History, and Divination For Beginners. The Peculiar Brunette. https://www.thepeculiarbrunette.com/ogham-rune-symbol-meanings-history-and-divination-for-beginners/

Brown, C. (2022, November 3). Celtic animism: How mythology can make you a more attentive traveler. Good Nature Travel Blog | Stories Are Made on Adventures; Natural Habitat Adventures. https://www.nathab.com/blog/celtic-animism-scotland/

Carr-Gomm, S. (2019, December 15). Tree meditation. Order of Bards, Ovates & Druids; OBOD. https://druidry.org/druid-way/teaching-and-practice/meditation/tree-meditation

Carr-Gomm, S. (2019, November 27). Tree lore. Order of Bards, Ovates & Druids; OBOD. https://druidry.org/druid-way/teaching-and-practice/druid-tree-lore

Carstairs, E. (2019, July 11). Ogham divination. Divination Lessons. https://divination-lessons.com/2019/07/11/ogham-divination/

Cartwright, M. (2021). Ancient Celtic religion. World History Encyclopedia. https://www.worldhistory.org/Ancient_Celtic_Religion/

Cartwright, M. (2021). Ancient Celts. World History Encyclopedia. https://www.worldhistory.org/celt/

Celtic deities. (2013, October 14). West Coast Pagan. https://westcoastpagan.com/celtic-reconstructionism/celtic-deities/

Celtic Gods. (n.d.). Mythopedia. https://mythopedia.com/topics/celtic-gods

Celtic mythology — Trees of The CloudForests —. (n.d.). Cloudforests. https://www.cloudforests.ie/trees-of-the-cloudforests/tag/celtic+mythology

Celtic Paganism History, Deities & Facts. (n.d.). Study.Com. https://study.com/academy/lesson/celtic-paganism-history-deities-facts-ancient-religion.html

Celtic Religion - what information do we really have. (n.d.). Murraystate.Edu. http://campus.murraystate.edu/academic/faculty/tsaintpaul/celtreli.html

Celtic tree calendar - my calendar land. (n.d.). Pravljice.org. https://www.pravljice.org/mycalendarland.com/calendar/yearly-calendars/celtic-tree-calendar

Celtic tree month of elder - November 25 - December 22. (n.d.). The Ethical Butcher. https://ethicalbutcher.co.uk/blogs/journal/celtic-tree-month-of-elder-november-25-december-22

Celts. (2017, November 30). HISTORY. https://www.history.com/topics/european-history/celts/

Choyt, M. (n.d.). Celtic culture - April: The Alder tree. Celticjewelry.com. https://www.celticjewelry.com/celtic-culture/alder-april

Choyt, M. (n.d.). Celtic culture - Cernunnos, the antlered god of power and blessing. Celticjewelry.com. https://www.celticjewelry.com/celtic-culture/cernunnos

Cross, J. (2019, November 18). Birch Tree meaning and magick. Sanctuary Everlasting. https://www.sanctuaryeverlasting.com/birch-tree-meaning-and-magick/

Dear, R. (1999). Celtic tree calendar: Your tree sign and you. Souvenir Press.

Derrig, J. (2022, July 27). A guide to Celtic Ogham symbols and their meanings. Theirishjewelrycompany.com. https://www.theirishjewelrycompany.com/blog/post/a-guide-to-celtic-ogham-symbols-and-their-meanings

EBK: Bran Fendigaid alias Bendigeitvran, God of Regeneration. (n.d.). Earlybritishkingdoms.com. https://www.earlybritishkingdoms.com/bios/bran.html

Ede-Weaving, M. (2021, May 24). Nature and the Celtic tree calendar. Order of Bards, Ovates & Druids. https://druidry.org/resources/nature-and-the-celtic-tree-calendar

Eilenstein, H. (2018). Cernunnos: Vom Schamanen zum Druiden Merlin. Books on Demand.

Evans, Z. t. (n.d.). Top 5 trees in Celtic mythology, legend and folklore. Folklorethursday.com. https://folklorethursday.com/legends/top-5-trees-in-celtic-mythology-legend-and-folklore/

Every Hawthorn tree has a story. (n.d.). The Present Tree. https://thepresenttree.com/blogs/tree-meanings/every-hawthorn-tree-has-a-story

Fee. (2021, January 18). Older than time: The myth of the Cailleach, the great mother. Wee White Hoose; Fee. https://weewhitehoose.co.uk/study/the-cailleach/

file-uploads/sites/2147611428/video/20407-4274-e6c6-3b2c-f6acf52be077_How_To_Make_An_Ogham_Set_-_Beginners_-_Lora_O_Brien_at_the_Irish_Pagan_School.mp4. (2023, February 2).

Gardiner, B. (2021, November 19). The best guide to understanding the wheel of the year. The Outdoor Apothecary. https://www.outdoorapothecary.com/the-wheel-of-the-year/

Gardiner, B. (2022, May 10). Litha: The incredible history, lore & 20 ways to celebrate. The Outdoor Apothecary. https://www.outdoorapothecary.com/litha/

Hidalgo, S. (2019, June 17). Tree ceremonies and guided meditations for working with the summer season. Llewellyn Worldwide. https://www.llewellyn.com/journal/article/2761

Hislop, I. (2021, April 28). The Celtic Tree of Life meaning & history. ShanOre Irish Jewelry; ShanOre Irish Jewelry. https://www.shanore.com/blog/the-celtic-tree-of-life-meaning-history/

Holly: Legends, customs, and myths. (n.d.). Psu.edu. https://extension.psu.edu/holly-legends-customs-and-myths

How to pronounce ostara? (n.d.). Pronouncenames.com. https://www.pronouncenames.com/Ostara

Irish Around The World. (2019, April 11). The Green Man – an ancient Celtic symbol of rebirth. Irish Around The World. https://irisharoundtheworld.com/the-green-man/

Irish Around The World. (2022, January 19). Top 20 Irish Celtic symbols and their meanings explained. Irish Around The World. https://irisharoundtheworld.com/celtic-symbols/

Irving, J. (2012). Ogham. World History Encyclopedia. https://www.worldhistory.org/Ogham/

Isabella. (n.d.). how to read ogham staves –. WytchenCrafts.

Jay, S. (2022, November 4). 14 Yule traditions & rituals to celebrate winter solstice. Revoloon. https://revoloon.com/shanijay/yule-traditions-rituals-to-celebrate-winter-solstice

Kay, K. (2014, March 17). What's your Celtic tree sign? Find out! Yahoo Life. https://www.yahoo.com/lifestyle/tagged/health/healthy-living/whats-celtic-tree-sign-152200321.html

Kelly, A. (2011, January 7). A month-by-month guide to the Celtic tree calendar – SEE PHOTOS. Irishcentral.com. https://www.irishcentral.com/roots/a-month-by-month-guide-to-the-celtic-tree-calendar-see-photos-113064709-237735251

Khaliela. (2022, February 2). Rowan meditation. Khaliela Wright. https://khalielawright.com/rowan-meditation/

King, J. (2019). Celtic warfare. World History Encyclopedia. https://www.worldhistory.org/Celtic_Warfare/

Lang, D. (2018, August 18). Ogham as a Practice. Esoteric Moment. https://esotericmoment.com/2018/08/18/ogham-as-a-practice/

LetsGoIreland. (2022, January 5). Celtic Symbols: Your complete guide to the Origins and meanings. Let's Go Ireland. https://www.letsgoireland.com/celtic-symbols-and-meanings/

LetsGoIreland. (2022, March 15). Celtic Tree of Life: Complete Guide to the Origin and Meaning. Let's Go Ireland. https://www.letsgoireland.com/celtic-tree-of-life/

LetsGoIreland. (2023, May 18). Celtic Tree of Life tattoo meaning and significance. Let's Go Ireland. https://www.letsgoireland.com/celtic-tree-of-life-tattoo-meaning/

LibGuides: Brigid: About. (2021). https://westportlibrary.libguides.com/brigid

LibGuides: Brigid: About. (2021). https://westportlibrary.libguides.com/brigid

Loh-Hagan, V. (2020). Celtic tree astrology. 45th Parallel Press.

Lor, H. O. (2021, September 24). The Tree of Life Symbol meaning. House Of Lor | Irish Jewellery | Pure Gold from Ireland; House of Lor Jewellery. https://houseoflor.com/the-tree-of-life-symbol/

Mark, J. J. (2019). Wheel of the Year. World History Encyclopedia. https://www.worldhistory.org/Wheel_of_the_Year/

Meditation with Trees. (n.d.). Viajealasostenibilidad.org. https://viajealasostenibilidad.org/meditation-with-trees/

Miller, F. P., Vandome, A. F., & McBrewster, J. (Eds.). (2010). Imbolc. Alphascript Publishing.

Month 3: Alder Tree Meditation. (n.d.). SoundCloud. https://soundcloud.com/nicola-mcintosh-52427282/alder-meditation

Mulhern, K. (n.d.). What is the Wheel of the Year? Patheos.com. https://www.patheos.com/answers/what-is-the-wheel-of-the-year

Neal, C. F. (2015). Imbolc: Rituals, recipes and lore for Brigid's day. Llewellyn Publications.

No title. (n.d.). Com.Eg. https://www.twinkl.com.eg/teaching-wiki/celtic-knot-meanings

No title. (n.d.). Study.com. https://study.com/learn/lesson/animism-beliefs-practices-thinking.html

No title. (n.d.). Twinkl.com. https://www.twinkl.com/teaching-wiki/the-celts

No title. (n.d.-a). Study.com. https://study.com/learn/lesson/yggrasil-tree-of-life.html

No title. (n.d.-b). Com.Eg. https://www.twinkl.com.eg/teaching-wiki/celtic-knot-meanings

O'Hara, K. (2023, January 2). The Morrigan: The story of the fiercest goddess in Irish myth. The Irish Road Trip. https://www.theirishroadtrip.com/the-morrigan/

O'Hara, K. (2023, June 1). Celtic Tree of Life (Crann Bethadh) meaning. The Irish Road Trip. https://www.theirishroadtrip.com/celtic-tree-of-life-symbol/

O'Hara, K. (2023a, May 29). 15 Celtic symbols and meanings (an Irishman's 2023 guide). The Irish Road Trip. https://www.theirishroadtrip.com/celtic-symbols-and-meanings/

O'Hara, K. (2023b, June 3). Trinity knot / Triquetra symbol: Meaning + history. The Irish Road Trip. https://www.theirishroadtrip.com/the-triquetra-celtic-trinity-knot/

Ogham alphabet. (n.d.). Omniglot.com. https://omniglot.com/writing/ogham.htm

Ogham Discipline: Understanding Your Connection. (n.d.). Ogham.Academy. https://www.ogham.academy/blog/ogham-discipline

Ogham Divination in The Summerlands. (n.d.). Summerlands.Com. http://www.summerlands.com/crossroads/library/oghamdiv.htm

Ogham Meditation Ritual. (2014, September 30). Ogham Divination. https://oghamdivination.wordpress.com/what-is-ogham/ogham-meditation-ritual/

Ogham: Ireland's original alphabet. (n.d.). Shamrock Gift. https://www.shamrockgift.com/blog/ogham/

Olsen, E. (2022, June 21). 13 Celtic Tree Months –. Celebrate Pagan Holidays. https://www.celebratepaganholidays.com/general/13-celtic-tree-months

Ostara (Spring Equinox) - the wiccan calendar -. (2017, June 13). Wicca Living. https://wiccaliving.com/wiccan-calendar-ostara-spring-equinox/

Ostara / spring equinox. (2015, August 16). By Land, Sea and Sky. https://thenewpagan.wordpress.com/ostara-spring-equinox/

Pagan, W. C. (2019a, June 14). Litha / Midsummer. West Coast Pagan. https://westcoastpagan.com/2019/06/13/litha-midsummer/

Pagan, W. C. (2019b, August 14). Lughnasadh / lammas. West Coast Pagan. https://westcoastpagan.com/2019/08/13/lughnasadh-lammas/

Pagan, W. C. (2019c, September 14). Mabon / autumn equinox. West Coast Pagan. https://westcoastpagan.com/2019/09/13/mabon-autumn-equinox/

Park, G. K. (2020). animism. In Encyclopedia Britannica.

Rajchel, D. (2015). Samhain: Rituals, Recipes & Lore for Halloween. Llewellyn Publications. https://thenewpagan.wordpress.com/wheel-of-the-year/samhain/

Rhys, D. (2021, August 13). Celtic sailor's knot - what does it symbolize? Symbol Sage. https://symbolsage.com/celtic-sailors-knot/

Rhys, D. (2021, July 29). Ogham symbols and their meaning - A list. Symbol Sage. https://symbolsage.com/ogham-symbols-and-their-meaning/

Rogador, C. (2020, June 28). The Celtic Triskele: History and meaning. Ireland Travel Guides. https://irelandtravelguides.com/celtic-triskele-history-meaning/

Rogador, C. (2021, June 9). The Celtic knots (different types and meanings). Ireland Travel Guides. https://irelandtravelguides.com/celtic-knot-history/

Sempers, C. (2002a). The Celtic tree calendar. Corvus Books.

Sempers, C. (2002b). The Celtic tree calendar. Corvus Books.

Silva, T. (2022, October 12). Alder tree symbolism and meanings. Grooving Trees. https://www.groovingtrees.com/alder-tree-symbolism

Sinclair, A. (2021, December 10). Celtic Tree Astrology: Zodiac signs & birthday horoscopes. Oak Hill Gardens. https://www.oakhillgardens.com/blog/celtic-tree-astrology-zodiac-signs-birthday-horoscopes

Soul, M. M. (2019). Imbolc: Witch's Journal & Workbook. Independently Published.

Stanton, K. M. (2022, December 1). Tree of Life meaning, symbolism, and mythology. UniGuide®; Kristen M. Stanton. https://www.uniguide.com/tree-of-life

Storey, L. (2018, October 19). Know a thing or two... Trees and druid traditions. The Simple Things. https://www.thesimplethings.com/blog/know-a-thing-or-two-trees-druid-traditions

Tailtiu: Harvest goddess. (n.d.). Goddess-pages.co.uk. https://goddess-pages.co.uk/galive/issue-18-home/tailtiu-harvest-goddess/

The Cauldron in Celtic life. (n.d.). Irelandseye.com. http://www.irelandseye.com/aarticles/culture/talk/superstitions/cauldron.shtm

The Celtic wheel of the year —. (n.d.). The Path of Integrity. https://thepathofintegrity.com/celtic-wheel

The Editors of Encyclopedia Britannica. (2018). Belenus. In Encyclopedia Britannica.

The Ogham alphabet. (n.d.). Ogham.Ie. https://ogham.ie/history/ogham-alphabet/

The Sacred Fire - Ancient Celtic Cosmology. (n.d.). Sacredfire.Net. https://www.sacredfire.net/cosmology.html

The Sacredness of Nature. (2012, March 22). The Druid Network.

The Song of Amergin: Modern English translation. (n.d.). Thehypertexts.com. http://www.thehypertexts.com/Song%20of%20Amergin%20Modern%20English%20Translation.htm

The tree meditation. (2013, May 2). The Druid Network.

The Tree of Life - an ancient Celtic symbol. (2021, September 26). Irish Urns. https://irishurns.com/the-tree-of-life-an-ancient-celtic-symbol/

Top 30+ Celtic symbols and their meanings (updated monthly). (n.d.). 1000logos.net. https://1000logos.net/top-30-celtic-symbols-and-their-meaning/

Traditions, I. (2016, July 24). Irish Traditions: The Celtic Tree of Life. Irish Traditions - A Tipperary Store; Irish Traditions. https://irishtraditionsonline.com/celtic-tree-of-life/

Tree of Life symbol: This image appears in many Irish expressions! (n.d.). Irish Expressions. https://www.irish-expressions.com/tree-of-life-symbol.html

We'Moon. (n.d.). Beltane rituals and traditions. We'Moon.

https://wemoon.ws/blogs/pagan-holiday-traditions/beltane

What's your tree sign according to Celtic tree astrology. (2015, September 23). Fantastic Gardeners Blog. https://blog.fantasticgardeners.co.uk/whats-your-tree-sign-according-to-celtic-tree-astrology/

Wheel of the Year. (2013, June 22). The Celtic Journey. https://thecelticjourney.wordpress.com/the-celts/wheel-of-the-year/

Who were the Celts? (n.d.). Twinkl. https://www.twinkl.com/teaching-wiki/the-celts

Who were the Druids? (2017, March 21). Historic UK. https://www.historic-uk.com/HistoryUK/HistoryofWales/Druids/

Wigington, P. (2008, June 2). The Celtic Ogham Symbols. Learn Religions. https://www.learnreligions.com/ogham-symbol-gallery-4123029

Wigington, P. (2008, June 2). The Celtic Ogham Symbols. Learn Religions. https://www.learnreligions.com/ogham-symbol-gallery-4123029

Wigington, P. (2011, September 18). Get to know the magic of the Celtic tree calendar. Learn Religions. https://www.learnreligions.com/celtic-tree-months-2562403

Wigington, P. (2014a, March 19). Beltane Rites and Rituals. Learn Religions. https://www.learnreligions.com/beltane-rites-and-rituals-2561678

Wigington, P. (2014b, June 21). Rites, rituals, and ways to celebrate Mabon, the autumn equinox. Learn Religions. https://www.learnreligions.com/mabon-rites-and-rituals-2562284

Will the real Lúnasa / Lughnasa / lughnasadh please stand up? (2010, August 1). Irish Language Blog | Language and Culture of the Irish-Speaking World; Irish Language Blog. https://blogs.transparent.com/irish/will-the-real-lunasa-lughnasa-lughnasadh-please-stand-up/

Williams, S. (2014, May 10). Celtic zodiac: Vine tree. Sun Signs. https://www.sunsigns.org/celtic-astrology-vine-tree/

Yule / Midwinter. (2015, August 27). By Land, Sea and Sky. https://thenewpagan.wordpress.com/wheel-of-the-year/yule-midwinter

www.ingramcontent.com/pod-product-compliance
Lightning Source LLC
Chambersburg PA
CBHW051850160426
43209CB00006B/1245